How to Land

That Big Idea—

and Other Secrets

of Creativity

in Business

The IdeaFisher

Marsh Fisher

Cofounder,

Century 21 Real Estate Corporation

PETERSON'S/PACESETTER BOOKS
PRINCETON, NEW JERSEY

Library of Congress Cataloging-in-Publication Data

Fisher, Marsh.
    The IdeaFisher : how to land that big idea—and other secrets of creativity in business / Marsh Fisher.
      p.   cm.
    Includes index.
    ISBN 1-56079-567-0
    1. Creative ability in business. 2. Creative thinking. 3. Association of ideas.
    4. Problem solving. I. Title.
    HD53.F57   1995
    650.1—dc20   95-19600
                                                        CIP

Creative direction by Linda Huber
Jacket design by Kathy Kikkert
Jacket illustration by Jean-François Podevin
Interior design by Cynthia Boone

Printed in the United States of America

10 9 8 7 6 5 4 3 2 1

Visit Peterson's Education Center on the Internet (World Wide Web) at http://www.petersons.com

Dedication

To my loving wife and partner, Marlee, without whom this book would *never* have been written.

Contents

P A R T 4

Fishing Tackle

Preface

Creativity is the only activity absolutely critical to the success of the human species. Its DNA is composed of ideas, which are at the heart of existence itself. Everything associated with progress comes from ideas, and they come from people using the proper tools and processes. No matter where they happen, new ideas and the waves they create will affect your job, your health, your prosperity, your world.

Nearly twenty-five years ago I had the idea for Century 21 Real Estate Corporation. My partner, Art Bartlett, and I cofounded that company in 1971; six years later I retired. For the next fifteen years I employed and worked with more than 200 researchers and scholars studying the process of thinking, the process of creativity.

Our research was based on these questions: How does the mind record information and how does it retrieve the words that comprise it? If we knew how or where words were recorded, would it be easier to find them? How would such a discovery be of any benefit?

What we learned proved very significant: The human mind records information by putting like things together. The mind doesn't store information as the dictionary does, that is, alphabetically, with "theater" under "T." "Theater" is actually stored together with all of its appropriate associations: tickets, show time, intermission, etc. We also discovered that in order to solve a problem, like "how to get to the theater," people have to recall every concept they can that is associated with "theater," e.g., directions, traffic, and parking. Recalling irrelevant information, such as, say, "life preservers," would do little to assist people in getting to the theater on time. This process is called Associational Thinking.

On the basis of this research I developed a tool, which has since been patented, that automates a part of the thinking process. In the same fashion as the human mind does, the IdeaFisher™ software program divides, stores, retrieves, and cross-references the English language and its concepts. It presents people with an almost infinite number of related words—information—that they can't always remember when they need to solve a problem. This relieves people of having to rely solely on their memories, allowing them to be creative at the touch of a key. IdeaFisher and its Add-On Modules also offer more than 10,000 questions broken down into specific tasks, such as creative writing; naming a new product; strategic planning; developing a marketing or public relations campaign; and helping to define or clarify any problem, and modify and evaluate any solution.

To test our findings, Dr. David L. Watson at the University of Hawaii conducted a study on the generation of ideas. Given the goal of developing cute or catchy phrases to print on a tee-shirt that had a picture of ducks playing in a Jacuzzi, two sets of people worked at producing ideas as long as they wished, but one group had lists of words from the IdeaFisher software that were associated with their task, and the other didn't. Those without the lists only worked an average of 55 minutes, when they "ran out of ideas." Those with the list worked an average of 78 minutes—a 42 percent increase.

There was also a statistical difference in the number of ideas produced. Those without the lists produced an average of 55 ideas. Those with them produced an average of 86 ideas—an increase of 56 percent.

After the test, subjects without the lists said they wanted to stop because they couldn't think of any more ideas. At that time, they were given the associated word lists, taught how to use them, and asked to continue working until they ran out of ideas again. On average they worked another 51 minutes and produced another 50 ideas—an increase of *90 percent* over the number of ideas that they first produced.

Dr. Watson concluded that even after they had exhausted themselves, people who activated their minds' natural Associational Thinking ability could work longer and produce a much larger number of ideas.

While the software program automates the mental process, this book is really an owner's manual to your mind, showing you how to get the most from it.

*   *   *

So how is this dynamic thing called "creativity" tamed and harnessed? How is the problem-solving process domesticated? How can you tap into and benefit from this incredible power?

Our research has proved that it is impossible to solve problems *without* Associational Thinking. If you remember nothing other than the fact that you think and solve problems by association, you will have a competitive edge over anyone who doesn't understand this process.

In the following pages I will share with you the results of our research: a process for consistently developing ideas, a process you can employ whether or not you're computer literate. For the first time, you'll learn how to use your mind's natural hierarchical system of storing and remembering knowledge to create a richer, more successful life.

No matter what type of problems you may be facing, practice this process every time you seek a solution or a new idea, and you'll be amazed at how easy it is. It will feel natural because it is. It's the same thinking process you've used all your life, only now you'll be able to activate it at will.

Reading through *The IdeaFisher,* you'll discover a unique blend of fiction and nonfiction designed to make learning the principle of Associational Thinking entertaining and easy. Each chapter builds on the preceding one to give you new and interesting ways to go angling for a great idea or a winning solution to a problem. You'll also discover how to use this principle to modify and evaluate your concept or solution.

The IdeaFisher is divided into four parts: The first short story of Part 1: Wading In introduces a character named the Captain, who interacts with a number of people in an office building. Each has a different story to tell, a different problem to solve. The Captain helps them all by utilizing the Principle of Associational Thinking. Chapter Two outlines the history of Associational Thinking, which stretches as far back as Aristotle. Part 2: Word Bait (Chapters Three to Ten) and Part 3: The Catch (Chapter Eleven) offer a unique format of short story, lesson, and exercise to help you learn how to solve a variety of problems, from developing a new product, organizing a fund-raiser, or writing a speech, to resolving an interpersonal conflict, creating a strategic plan, and developing an advertising campaign. Most importantly, you will learn the art of fishing for new concepts so you yourself can land the **Catch** . . . the Big Idea . . . the one that *didn't* get away.

In Part 4: Fishing Tackle, you'll find Bait Buckets, lists of associated words; SEAS, a hierarchial component the mind uses to store information; and a quick reference guide of more than 170 task-specific questions—Word Lures—you may turn to time and again to help solve problems. Throughout *The IdeaFisher* are brief excerpts—called Hook, Line & Sinker—of the experiences real-life business professionals had when they went angling for new ideas. A bibliography is included that lists both classical and contemporary treatments of Associational Thinking.

*   *   *

So will reading this book make *you* more successful? Well, your destiny, your future, will be constantly reshaped by new ideas. After learning how to capitalize on your own natural ability, you'll be able to leverage your creative talents to their fullest. Once you discover and utilize this secret, you'll be able to achieve your heart's desire, whether it's to get a corner office, win a pay raise, expand your business, or solve your problems.

To be consistently creative is to be empowered. There is nothing that can truly secure a better future for you than having the ability to be creative at will, to solve problems, and develop new concepts whenever needed. Creative people who understand the process of Associational Thinking and consistently employ it, will lead the way. You might as well be one of them.

And what if *everyone*'s ability to think and to solve problems were increased by just one-half of one percent? What if everyone learned how to consistently haul in the best ideas? Can you think of anything more wonderful, more exhilarating, or more rewarding? Could anything contribute more to individual happiness, or to the world's progress?

What if thinking, what if problem solving, became the centerpiece of the educational system? What if everything taught, all the text books for math, English, and history, were rewritten with the goal of supporting creative thinking? What if Associational Thinking, Thinking 101, were in every grade school at every level by the year 2000? What if creativity became a national obsession?

I guarantee you that children who learn the principle of Associational Thinking will be prepared for the future, prepared to navigate in fresh new waters with an unbeatable lead over their peers. Give your children the tools and processes with which to create the future, and they will.

Do you know the biblical saying that if you give a man a fish, you feed him for a day, but if you teach him how to fish, you feed him for a lifetime? If *you* want to be empowered with the ability to control your future and create a better tomorrow, then practice what you learn in *The IdeaFisher*.

Marsh Fisher
Cofounder of Century 21 Real
    Estate Corporation
Founder and Chairman of the Board
IdeaFisher Systems, Inc.
Irvine, California

Acknowledgments

Appreciation is first and foremost extended to the hundreds of people who worked for nearly two decades to create the IdeaFisher software. This book could not have been possible without their efforts.

Whereas if it weren't for Andrea Pedolsky, Executive Editor of Peterson's/Pacesetter Books, the book you are holding may well not be in your hands. My wife, Marlee, and I met Andrea in 1991, when this book was just . . . an idea. Since then, she has championed, and sometimes wrestled with, *The IdeaFisher*. However, through it all, she has expertly guided our effort. Every author should have an Andrea! Thank you, my friend. Recognition also goes to Jim Gish, Peterson's former Editor in Chief, Trade.

Bill Gladstone, our Literary Agent and the President of Waterside Productions, Inc., in Cardiff-by-the-Sea, California, is a walking rolodex. And thank heavens! His knowledge of the publishing industry, business acumen, and incredible depth of patience are the vital assets needed to bring any book into the printed page. Bill, you're the greatest! Thanks also to David Fugate.

Our copyright attorney, Jack Russo, of Russo & Hale in Palo Alto, California, has worked side by side with IdeaFisher Systems, Inc. for many years—and with good reason. Not only is he one of the sharpest people we know, he's one of the nicest too! Many thanks for your encouragement, Jack, and for overseeing the legal aspects of this project.

Special appreciation goes to our proofreading committee: George Truong and Chuck Yesson. Among the others who deserve public acknowledgment for their support of *The IdeaFisher* are: Mike Curtis, of Marine Biological Consultants; Pat Dugan of Furling & Rigging; Ed Good; John Hathaway of

Hathaway Enterprises; Palmer Jones (an incredible editor); LaLa Kinsey (a lifelong friend and a friend for life); Marsden Moran of Marsden Leverich Moran Architect; Ron Sargent; Rick Steck of the Royal Caribbean Cruise Line, and Maggie Stuckey.

The Cast

The Place

Cannery Village—a bayside turn-of-the-century fish-canning
facility that was transformed into a unique
blending of offices and shops.

The People

(in order of appearance)

Dirk, vice president, finance, Paris Lites Cosmetics Corporation
The Captain
Lenny, product development, Great Outdoors Apparel Company
Ted, product development, Great Outdoors Apparel Company
Regina, sales rep, Great Outdoors Apparel Company
Oscar Jacobs, divisional vice president, Great Outdoors Apparel Company
Senior Partner, Lynch, Cahn & Dodge
Monica Tietz, cofounder of Kuchen Kitchens International
Joshua Filipack, "currently in between opportunities"
Sylvie Simonait, proprietress of The Catch
Claudia Tochelle, CEO, Tochelle Travel, Inc.
Aunt Gina
Beryl Whitcomb, office manager, Tochelle Travel, Inc.
Francis Guerro, assistant to the CEO, Tochelle Travel, Inc.
Riccardo, finance manager, Tochelle Travel, Inc.
Saul Overend, sales manager, Tochelle Travel, Inc.
Harry, Joshua's roommate
Ian West, president, Marine Bank
CFO, Bernard Construction
Federico Hidalgo, property manager, Cannery Village
Yolanda Baccus, purchasing director, Fairweather & Co.
Tim Wallace Jr., president, Wallace and Son A.I.A.
Nick Stombolis, general contractor
Christian Stone, mechanical engineer
Herman Aune, retired purchasing director, Fairweather & Co.
Tim Wallace Sr., retired architect

Aaron Kozak, advertising director, Great Outdoor Apparel Company
Jack, copywriter, Great Outdoor Apparel Company
Monty, graphic artist, Great Outdoor Apparel Company
Zack Shipp, co-owner, A to Z Shelves, Inc.
Alfred, Woodrow co-owner, A to Z Shelves, Inc.

PART I

Wading In

O N E

Captain's Cleaning

Dirk was panicked . . .

Yanking at the Windsor knot, he pulled his tie from inside a vest damp with perspiration. Dirk's Brooks Brothers suit was taking on the harried look of its owner.

He had to come up with a new product name. His boss, Bob Beaumont, had offered a chunk of company stock to anyone who could name the cosmetics firm's new wrinkle cream by 5:00 p.m., and that was just half an hour away. The best the marketing department could do was "Preen Cream." Not exactly a suitable name for a revolutionary new product that removed wrinkles—forever.

Sitting at his desk, the new vice president of finance couldn't focus. He wasn't one of those "idea people," and he knew it. In fact, the only real thoughts running through his head were of a bright red Porsche and early retirement—both of which could be his once the Paris Lites Cosmetics Corporation went public and he sold his stock. But first he had to get his hands on that stock, and the quickest way to do that was to come up with a name.

Thinking a change of scenery would jump-start his neurons, Dirk walked over to the open window and gazed across Cannery Village's brick courtyard. A few years back, the turn-of-the-century fish cannery had been remodeled by developers into a charming U-shaped setting with elegant boutiques, antique shops, and restaurants topped by three floors of office space. Centered in the courtyard was a magnificent statue of Neptune standing astride a chariot of five playful dolphins balanced on an endless crest of waves that splashed into the reflecting pool below.

Dirk mentally eased his Porsche into fifth gear when the sound of scaffold winches jolted him from his reverie. He looked down and nearly fell over backwards as he spotted the face of a window washer moving up from the floor below.

"You're doing it incorrectly."

"Who—are you?" Dirk gasped.

"Captain's Cleaning at your command." Reassuring and strong, the voice came from somewhere inside a neat red beard streaked with gray that was attached to a gentleman obviously in good shape for his years. "I could not help overhearing your situation with Preen Cream," the Captain confessed, readjusting his bifocals.

"How did you ever hear about that? It's top secret. No one's supposed to know."

"No need for concern. Your secret is completely safe with me. And, if possible, I would like to help things along. When Preen Cream comes on the market, my stock in Paris Lites Cosmetics should skyrocket quite appreciably."

"*You* have stock?"

"Most assuredly. Haven't you?"

"But Preen Cream is inside information," Dirk replied, avoiding the Captain's question.

"Not to me, my friend. I am, after all, without question on the outside, am I not?" The Captain pointed to his scaffold. "And it is a bit of a habit of mine."

"What is?"

"Helping the good people who work in this building, such as yourself. I must admit the name *Preen Cream* leaves me a tad underwhelmed."

"Yeah, me too." Dirk was beginning to enjoy this engaging character with the kelly green suspenders and gentle manner.

"I overheard Bob's agitation this morning over the marketing department's suggested name. Since then, I have been listening to you most of the afternoon."

"You've been *what*?"

"I listen to all the good people in Cannery Village. And I must say it has been a marvelous experience. My investment holdings have increased a hundredfold since I began." The Captain rubbed his beard. "Speaking of which, what do you propose to do about Preen Cream?"

Relaxing a bit, Dirk rested his elbows on the window sill. "Beats me. I'm good at negotiating. I'm good at getting things done. But I'm a lousy idea person. No matter how hard I try, my brain just doesn't cooperate. I focus on the problem, but my mind always starts to wander. So when I can't get an idea, I take a break, go for a walk, maybe have a bite to eat. But to tell you the truth, I'm really just hoping like mad that something brilliant will pop into my mind."

"Pop into your mind? That's leaving a lot to chance, isn't it?" asked the Captain. "Actually, your only problem is that you don't understand the process of consistently reeling in ideas. Great ideas will not simply jump into your boat because you need them. However, there is a process for consistently coaxing them in and it's based on how people think . . . using the right Word Bait and all."

"Word Bait? What's that?"

"It's part of the process I tell people about to help them to see more clearly." The Captain gestured to his squeegee and cleaning solutions. "Think of it as my job description."

Dirk smiled. "At this point, I'll try anything. That wall clock over there likes to remind me that I'm about to lose the deal of a lifetime." The clock obliged with a punctual tick as another minute disappeared. "If you have the time to teach me, I'll find the time to learn. And I'm talking right now!"

"My pleasure," said the Captain, preparing to raise his scaffold to Dirk's floor. "By all means."

Then, for the first time in his life, Dirk began to learn how to consistently get new ideas: how to fish for them.

Securing his lines alongside Dirk's window, the Captain continued, "It is undeniably true that upon occasion good ideas might come to us quickly and quite unannounced. If you have ever said 'the light bulb just went off,' you were referring to an inspiration from out of the blue. However, that's merely magical inspiration, which is anything but dependable. In order to be able to come up with ideas, good ideas, consistently, to meet a deadline—"

"Now twenty-three minutes away," Dirk interrupted, looking over at the clock.

"—or complete your employer's assignment, or whatever the need may be, you must be able to be creative on demand."

"Ain't that the truth?" Dirk mumbled, dropping into his chair.

"The human mind, my friend, is truly a wondrous thing. You *can* come up with ideas whenever you want them—they're *already stored in your brain*. All that is needed is a process for accessing them. And fortunately, there is just such a process. It's your mind's own way of working. And it's called Associational Thinking." The Captain pointed toward the courtyard. "Take a moment and look at that fountain."

Dirk shifted uneasily. "Excuse me, no offense intended, but now I've only got twenty-two minutes. Can we just skip the fountain and get down to business?"

"I empathize with your feelings. However, it's most important that you understand the foundation of this process so you may use it efficiently in the moments that remain. You see, all the information you have ever encountered is stored in your memory, separated into categories. These categories contain words—concepts, if you will—that are, in some fashion, associated with one another. When you attempt to solve a problem, or come up with an idea, your mind automatically turns to the right category. For instance, the person who designed that fountain had to consider such concepts as water, granite, size, and texture. Considering a concept such as typewriter would have done little to help with the problem of designing a fountain. Are you beginning to understand?"

"Maybe."

"Delightful," said the Captain. "And the more closely associated words or concepts that the designer could remember from those specific categories, the quicker she was able to design a better fountain. Is that a little clearer?"

"I think so."

"Now, unfortunately, at any given time, people can only remember a limited number of associated words. To retrieve all the words that are directly associated with a problem, not just some of them, they need to be able to lure them from their memory."

"Yeah, but—"

"To put it more simply, Dirk, the ability to develop new ideas is only limited by your ability to remember all those associated concepts already stored in your mind. You simply have to learn how to ask for them. Or, as I like to think of it: How to *fish* for them.

"Your answer always lies right in there," said the Captain, pointing just beneath Dirk's thatch of thinning hair. "Well, time is running out, my friend. If you intend to meet your deadline, I would be more than happy to assist you in fishing for a few new concepts."

"You got it! What do we do first?"

"First, you simply take a blank piece of paper that we will call your Bait Bucket. And what do you suppose we will put into your Bait Bucket?"

"Words, I guess."

"What type of words?"

"Words associated with my problem of renaming Preen Cream."

"Exactly! That's Word Bait, words closely associated with your problem. And the more words—Word Bait—the merrier. You never know what type of Word Bait will land the Catch . . . the Big Idea. To land the Big Idea, you must take ample Word Bait from your Bait Bucket, put it on your hook, and cast it into a category of associated words. Once you pull up your Big Ideas you might store them in your Idea Creel and later on modify and evaluate them, deciding which ones are best and which ones to throw away." The Captain straightened his suspenders. "Shall we begin?"

Dirk was starting to get the drift of the whole thing. "You bet."

"Splendid," responded the Captain. "Now list a few words from the problem itself. They'll be your initial Word Bait."

Dirk thought out loud a minute. "Develop a name for the company's face cream. That's the problem. So I guess name, company, face, and cream are my initial Word Bait, right?"

"Right you are. What do those words bring to mind?"

"Well, wrinkles is a pretty obvious one." Dirk jotted it down. "And old. And how about Paris Lites, the name of our company?"

"Excellent choices," said the Captain. "Now you have three larger pieces of Word Bait—wrinkles, old, and Paris Lites. The next step is to use each of these to fish a little deeper, to find even bigger Word Bait."

Dirk started to think again, this time about wrinkles. "Women associate wrinkles with aging. Women without wrinkles look young."

"You see? The first piece of bigger Word Bait, wrinkles, made you think of young, which is an even larger piece of Word Bait. And how could you use young to solve your problem?"

"Well, let's see. Every woman wants to look young. Young what?" Dirk sat up straight. "Oh, I know! **YOUNG AGAIN** . . . Wow! That's a lot better than Preen Cream."

"Infinitely better. Now try another piece of your Word Bait and see where that leads you."

Next Dirk thought about old, which made him think of ancient, ageless, forever, and . . . "Wait a minute . . . Why not . . . **ETERNAL** . . . or **ETERNITY**?" Dirk laughed, "Hey, I just landed two more!"

"Try once again," said the Captain.

Dirk tried Paris Lites. Bob picked that name for his cosmetics company because most people imagined Paris at night to be the most romantic spot in the world, and "Lights" when spelled "Lites" referred to the cosmetic's texture.

What did Paris make Dirk think of? Well, that song, "I love Paris in the Springtime." *Springtime*! Now, how could he use Springtime with his problem? Springtime meant . . . it meant, fresh, alive, renewed . . . perfect for a cream that offered all of the same! And better yet . . . "**SPRINGTIME BY PARIS LITES!** Bob will *love* it," shouted Dirk.

This was great. In just a few minutes, four excellent names had jumped into Dirk's Idea Creel. He looked up at the Captain. "Why didn't I think of these before?"

"Simply because you did not understand the process for consistently bringing in new ideas. Just now, however, you asked your mind to respond through Associational Thinking. You fished for new concepts in just the right way. When you threw in your Word Bait, you immediately remembered other words—more and bigger Word Bait. And for each of them, even though you may not have been consciously aware of it, you asked yourself two questions: 'What does this word make me think of?' And, 'How can I use this word to solve my problem?' "

The Captain explained that just as there are a variety of ways to attract the big bass that lurk beneath a riverbank ledge waiting for the right bait, there are a variety of different ways, such as using question lures, OCEANS, SEAS, and TIDE POOLS, and comparing, to gather Word Bait that will, in turn, attract ideas . . . Big Ideas.

Glancing at the clock, the Captain said, "Usually, at this point we would continue on to the next steps—take a good look at your Catch, modify and evaluate each idea, decide which to keep and which to throw back. Unfortunately, your deadline is near, so I must return another day to chat about those." Preparing to ascend to the fourth floor, the Captain added, "Best of Luck!"

A loud tick brought Dirk back to reality. Two minutes left. He straightened his tie, checked his hair in the mirror next to the bookcase, put on his jacket, and tucked the sheet of paper with **Young Again**, **Eternal**, **Eternity**, and **Springtime BY PARIS LITES** under his arm.

"These may not get me the stock bonus," he mused as he glanced back at the window, "but they're a heckuva lot better than Preen Cream. And to think, they all came from <u>wrinkles</u>, <u>old</u>, and <u>Paris</u> <u>Lites</u>! Fishing, huh? That Captain guy is really onto something."

Visions of early retirement—and that red Porsche—in his head, Dirk closed the door behind him, leaving the clock to tick on alone.

T W O

Associational
Thinking from
Aristotle to . . .

Although it took a twentieth-century "window-washer" to
enlighten Dirk on the process . . . various aspects of
Associational Thinking were contemplated as early as the fifth
century B.C. by Plato and then Aristotle. It wasn't until the
seventeenth century A.D., however, that the concept was given
a solid foundation, when English philosopher John Locke and a
group of theorists called Associationists undertook the task of
developing a theory to explain the thought process.[1]

Before that time, thinking was commonly assumed to be mostly
a function of intuition. It was believed that the mind received
information through the five senses of sight, smell, touch, taste,
and sound, which it then somewhat carelessly stored. When a
person thought of a concept, something mysterious occurred in
his mind and an image was somehow brought to his attention
from deep within his memory. In short, the process of thinking
was viewed as dependent upon luck, chance, maybe even fate.

This explanation didn't satisfy Locke and the Associationists.
They asked why it was that when a person heard the voice of a
friend in a dark room, his mind created an image of that friend.
Why was it that when someone walked in the woods and
smelled the smoke from a hearth, he would sometimes be

---

[1] Gates, Elmer. *Art of Mind-Using*. New York: Exposition Press, 1971.

reminded of his own home and of days long since past, when he sat before a fire on a cold winter evening? How could these experiences be explained?

Memory Triggers

Locke's followers reasoned that one way to explain these experiences would be if concepts, the building blocks of information, were stored in the mind not in isolation from one another but within groups. Each group would consist of concepts that were associated with one another, like members of a family. If that was so, then knowledge consisted of joining and separating these concepts according to what they had in common. The reason why the smell of smoke acted as a trigger and caused someone to recall his own past in detail was that his strongest memory of that smell was associated in his mind with the other memories of his own home and hearth. Since these concepts were originally presented to that person through his senses as being associated with each other, his mind stored them in the same way.

This is Associational Thinking—the principle that any concept leads to other concepts through a process of triggering groups of associated information.

William James, considered America's foremost philosopher-psychologist in the last 150 years, challenged people to be silent for a moment and then to command themselves to "Remember! Recollect!" In doing so, they were unable to bring any concrete image to their minds. In his book *Talks to Teachers*,[2] James explained that people couldn't *think* because they didn't know *what* they were to *remember*. Their memories needed a *cue*, a *trigger*, such as the word breakfast, around which they could gather other associated concepts like coffee, eggs, and bacon. Then, and only then, could they *think*.

Try it yourself. Try to remember—nothing. Does your mind lock up? Are you unable to *think*? Of course, because, as James said, "The art of remembering is the art of thinking."

Now, try this: Consider a word that represents an object, activity, or concept with which you're familiar. Focus on that concept or the image that it represents . . . just *think* about it. Let your thoughts go, and see what happens.

Like most people, you'll probably find that your mind naturally and automatically begins to call up several other concepts or images that are associated with your original thought. One concept will always remind you of others, since every concept that comes to you, via your senses, is immediately sent into your memory where it makes connections with the other concepts already there. *The result of this activity is called thinking.*

In his book *The Society of Mind*,[3] the acknowledged father of Artificial Intelligence, Marvin Minsky, explains the process this way: "When our Redness, Touch, or Toothache agents send their signals to our brains, each by itself can only say, 'I'm here.' The rest of what such signals 'mean' to us depends on how

----

[2] James, William. *Talks to Teachers*. New York: W. W. Norton & Company, Inc., 1900, p. 87.

[3] Minsky, Marvin. *The Society of Mind*. New York: Simon & Schuster, 1986, p. 113.

they're linked to all our other agencies. In other words, the 'qualities' of signals sent to brains depend only on relationships.''

For example, when you consider an "apple," you remember more than just a colored orb. You might recall a particular color, perhaps several of them, a context or environment— maybe an orchard or a grocery store bin, or simply your hand holding an apple. If you take a bite, a myriad of other thoughts will be produced—concepts that have been stored together with your original concept of an apple that will be waiting in the background of your memory to be recalled each time you see another apple.

Just what concepts are stored in your memory along with "apple" depends upon your own unique experience of apples. If, for example, you once took a bite of an apple and found a worm, the memory cluster in which the experience is stored would contain different concepts and images than if the apple had been ripe and free of worms. Likewise, if you happen to find the taste of an apple terrible, your memory cluster would be different from that of a person who thinks apples taste great.

Regardless of what your particular and unique experience of apples happens to be, the concept of apples stored in your memory is surrounded by many other concepts, each of which is somehow related to apples as you have experienced them in the past. In other words, each person has a unique memory cluster that has the concept of "apple" at its center.

In 1992, scientists discovered physical evidence that confirmed the theory that the brain does indeed store information in categories—hierarchical categories. In their research of brain tumor patients, the distinguished Neurology and Cognitive

Science Departments of Johns Hopkins proved that there actually are certain brain cell clusters dedicated to specific categories of concepts such as plants, animals, and emotions. To date, upwards of twenty different categories, the brain's own natural categories for knowledge, have been identified. Within these particular categories, the researchers found that patients had stored appropriate associations, such as green with plants, cow with animals, and anger with emotions. Further, they discovered that humans have multiple representations of the same things in their brain; that in order to think about a cow, a thinker must go to his category of animal to come up with such associations as color and size.[4]

The discovery that the brain physically organizes knowledge through a distinct system, putting information (words and concepts) into categories—even more importantly, hierarchical categories—took Associational Thinking out of the realm of theory and put it solidly into the realm of principle.

Imagination Is Combination

Although John Locke said that people's concepts originate through their sensory experience, there are some concepts that can't be explained in that way alone. Consider a unicorn, for example. Unicorns don't really exist. They never did. So how can the concept of a unicorn be explained?

Associational Thinking solves the puzzle. In addition to storing ideas in associated groups, there is another function of the mind

---

[4] Hilts, Philip J. " 'Hole' in Tumor Patient's Memory Reveals Brain's Odd Filing System," *The New York Times*, September 15, 1992. *Nature Magazine*, September 1992.

called imagination. Imagination has access to all of the stored information, and it has the ability to pick and choose images and concepts from different groups and combine them.

For example, you most likely have the concept of a horse and a beast with horns in your memory because you've actually experienced these things in some way. If you wish, you can put your imagination to work on these concepts and combine them so that you end up with an entirely new concept—the concept of a horse with horns or one horn. And that, according to the principle of Associational Thinking, is precisely how the concept of a unicorn was created.

The concept—the mental image—of a unicorn is a combination of other concepts. It's a mental construction put together by imagination out of the basic building blocks that are stored in memories.

Thinking Is Associating

Thinking, which had originally been thought of as intuition, is now understood to be the result of contemplating the relationship between two concepts; for example, eggs and bacon will cause you to think of breakfast. According to Locke, who believed that the mind is essentially an associating machine, "The connecting *is* the thinking."

Reiterating Locke's assumption, Marvin Minsky noted that "The secret of what anything means to us depends on how we've connected it to all the other things we know. . . . A thing with just one meaning has scarcely any meaning at all. . . . But well-connected meaning-structures let you turn ideas around in your mind to consider alternatives and envision things from many perspectives until you find one that works. And that's what we mean by thinking!"[5]

Creativity Is New Relationships

Any new idea is the recombination of past experiences that form new associations. New associations, the essence of creativity, come from borrowing, adding to, or otherwise manipulating old concepts and their associations with those of other concepts.

Creativity is a four-step process that happens quite naturally. First, you have to record concepts by putting them into your memory. Then you must be able to remember them. Next, you reassociate or rearrange those concepts to form combinations. For instance, combining "tomato" with "spherical" gives you the thought of a "tomato's shape." That's thinking: making relationships. The fourth step is to make brand-new relationships between the concepts and their associations. Combining the concept of "tomato" with that of "spherical" gave an entrepreneur the new thought of developing a square tomato, which would be easier to pack and ship. That's creative thinking.

Remembering Is Key

Remembering concepts and their associations is the key to thinking and creativity. Creative people are not necessarily

---

[5] Minsky, Marvin. *The Society of Mind.* New York: Simon & Schuster, 1986, p. 64.

those who have recorded the most in their memories, only those who can remember the most from their memories. A concept must first be remembered before it can be contemplated.

The more possibilities you can trigger and the more concepts you can recall, the better your chances are of coming up with an idea or a solution. However, every human mind comes fully equipped with a censor, which is a good thing, because without this censor, which restricts direct access to all but a small portion of your memories at any given time, you would be overcome with memories. For instance, whenever you walked into a restaurant your mind would be flooded with all the memories of past restaurants you've experienced—all the food you ate, all the people you met, every chair you sat in. It would be like setting off a nuclear chain reaction of memories. On the other hand, this also means you can't remember all of the concepts associated with restaurant, or any other word, whenever you want them.

In order to remember, your mind utilizes the associational method it used to store a concept in the first place. Accordingly, the more your effort to remember parallels *how* a concept was originally stored, and the closer that concept is to a specific problem, the more successful your effort will be to create its solution. That's why triggers (Word Bait), such as "breakfast," that are themselves associated with the concepts you are trying to remember, are so important. Using triggers, you can easily retrieve associated concepts and images, shifting and recombining their elements to discover new ideas.

The retrieval aspect of Associational Thinking is the most important element of all, for it provides a powerful stimulus to creativity, problem solving, and the generation of new ideas. Once you learn how to retrieve all the concepts you have stored in the "back of your mind," you'll be able to be consistently creative. You'll say to yourself, "Well, of course! I knew it all the time." And it's true! You just had to bring it to the surface.

Or, as William James said, "Each [concept] is a hook to which [the original impression] hangs, a means to fish it up when sunk below the surface."[6]

---

[6] Op. Cit., James.

PART 2

Word Bait

T H R E E

New Socks:
Product
Development

"So who is this Captain guy?" Lenny asked.

"Just the best idea guy in the business," said Ted.

"And the funny thing is he's not even *in* our business," added Regina.

"You mean he doesn't work for the Great Outdoors Apparel Company?" asked Lenny, the firm's latest addition to its product development team.

The rest of the group smiled at one another. They were on their way to an afternoon meeting in hopes of developing a new product concept for the company's outdoor clothing line that would spur the historically lagging summer sales.

"New employees can be so . . . so very new," chortled the divisional VP Oscar Jacobs as he led the group into the conference room. "I'll show you the ropes, Lenny," he offered, pointing toward the scaffolding lines that framed the window.

Oscar's humor could be a tad obtuse to the unsuspecting, thought Regina.

Everyone settled in around the table. "What I meant was," said Ted, "as far as Oscar and I are concerned, he's the best guy in the idea business. And, since it's our job to come up with a sure-fire new product, we asked the Captain to join us this morning and lend a hand.''

"I heard a story about him,'' said Regina, the 28-year-old hotshot from the sales division who had also been asked to join the team's effort. "He's a friend of a guy I know at the cosmetics company on the third floor. He just hung outside, talking to Dirk about something called Word Bait and how to use it to fish for new concepts. Dirk said it really helped him come up with some terrific names for a new product.''

"What?'' Lenny was incredulous. "You gotta be joking.''

"The joke is most definitely on people who do not understand the process of consistently developing ideas and solutions to problems.'' The voice came from outside. All eyes turned toward the window as the rising scaffolding brought the Captain into view.

Lenny just stared.

"Pleased to meet you, Lenny and Regina,'' the Captain said, taking a small bow. "And, as always, it's a pleasure to see my old friends Ted and Oscar, with whom I have spent many a delightful afternoon angling for new ideas.'' Regina glanced at Lenny, silently enjoying his look of disbelief.

"Let me explain myself by asking you a question if I may, Lenny,'' said the Captain.

"Sure.''

"Have you ever gone fishing?''

"Now and then.''

"Then, you are aware of the need to bait your hook, correct?"

"Sure."

"And upon occasion you may use tiny fish as bait for larger fish?"

"Yeah, sure. Like minnows and stuff."

"Splendid! And, all things considered, fishing for fish is simply a process, isn't it? You bait your hook, cast your line, and try to land your Catch. And, should you come up empty, you move to a new spot or try different bait—or perhaps both. Well, fishing for new concepts is virtually the same thing. Except, rather than use little fish for bait, we use words."

"Words?"

"Most definitely! You see, concepts and ideas are the same thing. They are the building blocks of what we call information," answered the Captain. "In other words, how do we communicate information to one another?"

Lenny thought for a moment. "With words!"

"Exactly," said the Captain. "Concepts, ideas, information, and words are really all one and the same thing. Take the result of this afternoon's meeting as an example. With a little good luck fishing, when this meeting comes to a close, you will write a report describing your Catch—your Big Ideas for a new summer clothing product. And that report will use words to express your ideas. Therefore, one of the first steps in developing new ideas is to simply recall as many words as possible."

"And the real key to angling for ideas is Word Bait," added Oscar. "Words that are closely associated with the problem."

"Right you are, my friend."

"Oh!" said Regina. "Now I get it. When Dirk told me about Word Bait, I figured he only had one oar in the water. But you're just using words to fish for . . . to find more words because . . . because words and ideas are the same thing!"

"That they are!" said the Captain. "Some of the small fish—the first Word Bait you think of—are really like anchovies, or 'minnows and stuff,' as Lenny pointed out. You'll use them as triggers to attract even more words a little higher on the food chain. Perhaps a mackerel you could then use to land that really Big Catch—that Big Idea for your summer clothing line.

"Now, our minds actually think by associating one concept with another. By associating the concept of apple with the concept of red, we have the thought of the color of the apple. This is called Associational Thinking and we do it naturally all day long. Concepts and ideas, information if you will, such as apple are stored in our memory by categories. These categories are filled with concepts closely associated with one another. Therefore, apple and red are stored together in the category of fruit.

"To come up with great ideas, you simply need to use Word Bait and go fishing in the right categories. Think of it as fishing in an OCEAN, a SEA, or perhaps, even a TIDE POOL."

"But, but how do we come up with Word Bait in the first place, let alone figure out where to fish with it?" asked Lenny.

"It's like Oscar said," added Ted. "We have to start with words that are closely associated with the problem. You know, we can find an ocean of words in any dictionary or thesaurus, and with lots of searching, we'll eventually find some words that are related to our specific problem. But they're not listed by how closely associated they are with each other—they're just words swimming around in alphabetical circles. So, we need to focus on our problem and come up with a list of words that have some direct association with it. Then, we go fishing in the same category that those words are stored in.''

''Huh?''

''Okay, Lenny, I'll tell you what,'' said Oscar. ''Look at it this way. We're trying to develop a new clothing product for summer. So, that's what we should concentrate on, not something irrelevant like electrical wall plugs.''

''Right,'' said Ted. ''Thinking about electrical wall plugs might eventually lead us to a Big Idea, but it's also going to waste a lot of time.''

''Let's give it a try,'' said Regina.

''Wonderful,'' said the Captain as he sat down on the broad window sill. ''Now, *Step One* is to clearly define the problem, which you have already done by deciding that you need to develop a new outdoor clothing product for summer. This gives you your initial Word Bait of outdoor clothing and summer. *Step Two* is coming up with as many words as you can that are related to those concepts while keeping the problem you are trying to solve in mind. *Step Three* is simply asking two Word Bait Questions of each minnow you've hooked. First: What does this word make me think of? And, second: How can I use this word—alone, some part of it, or in combination with another—to solve my problem? Your answers to these questions will give you even more and bigger Word Bait. Simply repeat the process until you pull in the Catch.''

''If we're on Step Two, does each of us come up with a list or do we work together?'' Lenny asked Oscar.

"Why not both ways?" responded Oscar.

"Puh-lees, we'll be here forever," said Regina.

"Then," said the Captain, "in the interest of time, perhaps it would be best if each of you took a minute and independently wrote down as many pieces of Word Bait as you can think of. Do not attempt to land that Big Idea on your first cast. Simply gather together some words associated with outdoor clothing and summer."

"Ya got a deal," said Oscar, reaching for his pen and legal pad.

The Captain announced, "Now begin!"

The group began to write down the words that came to mind. After sixty seconds, the Captain said, "Time's up! Ted, why don't you collect all the papers and write the minnows on the marker board."

Ted picked up the papers and approached the board. Finding the black marker, he wrote:

Regina—
Outdoor Clothing
new product
increase summer sales
bigger commissions 4 me
designer suits 4 me
Saks Fifth Avenue 4 me
THIS is not solving
the problem

"A valiant first effort," the Captain said to Regina. "However, look at what you actually did. By writing down increase summer sales, you merely restated the problem. That is not fishing for new concepts. To truly go fishing, you need Word Bait. Your list merely addresses the need for finding a solution—landing the Big Catch. And, for that very reason, you didn't.''

"I see. I got off track. But how do I get back on track?" she asked.

"We'll attend to that in a moment," responded the Captain. "Perhaps first we should best review the other lists."

Ted returned to the board and wrote:

```
Ted—
Summer
hot in town
sweaty
buggy
mosquitoes
```

"Well done. You listed a number of words that are associated with your initial Word Bait, thereby creating even bigger Word Bait. Shall we try Lenny's list next?"

Lenny's eyes searched his notepad, wondering how much longer he'd be employed by the Great Outdoors Apparel Company, as Ted wrote:

```
Lenny—
summer
this is dumb
what did I do for
my summer vacation?
looked for a job
keep looking
```

All eyes hit the ceiling except Lenny's, which were now searching his shoes.

"That's all right, Lenny," said the Captain. "As Regina did, you wrote down a list of loosely associated words. However, you did not keep them specifically related to the problem, so, therefore, they're not Word Bait. In other words, they would not do much to increase summer sales for the company that employs you."

"Employed me," corrected Lenny.

"There simply isn't any reason to feel bad, my friend," said the Captain. "You are learning a new process, and that is what's important."

"Let's see what Oscar came up with," said Ted.

Oscar—
Outdoor Clothing
hats
coats
pants
shoes
socks

The Captain turned toward the group. "Oscar wrote down words that are indeed associated with the Word Bait from your problem. Now notice that everyone's list reveals how the mind really works. By associating one concept with another, you each developed a number of new concepts."

"Yeah, like a new job," murmured Lenny.

"Some of those concepts," the Captain continued, "were not as . . . vibrant as others."

"So the more concepts . . . words, I mean Word Bait we can come up with the better," said Lenny.

The Captain smiled in approval. "Exactly."

"And," Lenny continued, "the more closely that Word Bait is associated to the problem—"

"The sooner you'll have the solution!" chimed in Regina.

"And that, my dear Regina, is how you stay on track," noted the Captain.

"Angling for new ideas is really just working with your mind the way it works itself," she concluded. Regina turned to the Captain. "This sounds great. Let's go fishing!"

And that they did. After the Captain advised them not to be concerned with technical feasibility at this point but only with landing the Big Idea, the group selected Oscar's Word Bait list to try out Step Three. Ted returned to the board once again.

Outdoor Clothing
hats
coats
pants
shoes
socks

The Captain guided them by asking, "What does hat make you think of?"

"My Uncle Russell," said Ted. "He always wore a bowler."

"How could you use that to solve the problem of creating a new line of outdoor clothing to increase summer sales?"

Everyone watched Ted. "You got me."

"Next," Oscar groaned.

"What does <u>coats</u> make you think of?" asked the Captain.

As each of them joined in, they began to shout out words so fast that Ted could barely keep pace.

"<u>Cold</u>"

"<u>Winter</u>"

"<u>Parkas</u>"

"<u>Long</u> <u>coats</u>"

"<u>Short</u> <u>coats</u>"

"<u>Top</u> <u>hat</u> and <u>tails</u>"

"Top hat and tails?"

"I'm free-associating Regina, don't interrupt."

"You're doing what, Lenny?"

"Oh . . . yeah. Keep it specific to the problem."

The Captain suggested they try a new word. "How could you use <u>cold</u> to solve the problem?"

"We could develop a <u>cold</u>-weather coat, but we already manufacture one."

"Next!"

"<u>Pants</u> make me think of that heavy <u>material</u> used in <u>hunting</u> <u>pants</u>."

"Yeah, it's nearly as good as <u>leather</u>."

"How could you use <u>leather</u> to solve the problem?" the Captain asked.

"Hey, why not <u>leather</u> <u>hunting</u> <u>pants</u> for winter?"

"Could you combine <u>leather</u> <u>hunting</u> <u>pants</u> with something else to solve the problem?"

"*I* know!" shouted Oscar. "<u>Safety</u> is a big part of hunting, so why not **fluorescent leather hunting pants**?"

Applause and laughter filled the room. "We landed a Big One that time!"

"But I thought we were trying to increase *summer* sales," reflected Lenny.

"Oops."

"That's no problem. I'll just put it in our Idea Creel for the future," said Ted, as he pulled out a piece of fresh paper to keep track of their new ideas. "Let's keep going."

At last they reached <u>shoes</u> and <u>socks</u> at the end of Oscar's list. The board was covered with words, but the original problem remained unsolved.

The Captain crossed his arms and waited. The four at the table looked at one another and then at the Captain. Finally, Regina spoke up. "I think we're stuck."

"Then perhaps you should find another fishing hole," suggested the Captain. "Remember the second Word Bait Question?"

"How can we use one piece of Word Bait, either by itself, or some part of it, to help solve our problem," offered Lenny.

"Exactly! And the last part of that question was, how can one piece of Word Bait be combined with another?" The Captain suggested that next they try comparing two very different pieces of Word Bait.

Skipping to the end of Oscar's Word Bait list, they chose socks again. And since summer was a key ingredient of their problem, Ted cleared off the board and wrote socks next to his list of Word Bait that included:

Summer	Socks
hot in town	
sweat	
buggy	
mosquitoes	

The Captain began, "What does hot in town make you think of compared to socks?"

"Light socks"

"No socks"

"How can you use light socks or no socks with your problem?"

"No socks, no product," said Ted.

"No product, no sales, no fat IRA account," said Regina.

"No fat IRA account, no trips abroad, no house at the Cape—"

"Ah, Captain," interjected Oscar. "Until Regina and Ted rejoin us, how about moving forward?"

"A superb idea! What does <u>sweat</u> make you think of compared to <u>socks</u>?"

"The boys' locker room on Sunday afternoon."

"But you're a girl! How could you—"

"Hold on, Lenny, Regina's got a point. Sweaty socks really <u>smell</u>."

"How can you use <u>smell</u> with the problem of developing a new clothing product for summer?" asked the Captain.

"Hey, that's simple," said Oscar. "A new **sock** that's **smell proof**!"

"Good going, Oscar. You landed one!" Everyone reached across the table to shake his hand.

"What's next?"

<u>Buggy</u> and <u>mosquitoes</u>.

"Pretty much the same," conceded Ted. "Let's go with <u>mosquitoes</u>."

"As good a choice as any," said the Captain. "Now, here is the final question. What does <u>mosquitoes</u> make you think of compared to <u>socks</u>?" The answers came flying back.

"Invisible"

"Outdoors"

"Camping"

"Travel in pairs"

"So do socks"

"Write faster, Ted!"

"Loud . . . buzzing"

"Stings"

"Bites"

"Calamine lotion"

"Insect repellent"

"I got it!" Regina shouted. Everyone turned, half expecting to see a dead bug in her outstretched hand.

"Insect repellent socks!"

The group fell silent as Regina slid back in her chair. The Captain bowed. "That's the biggest one we landed yet," gasped Ted. "Unbelievable. Great work, Regina!"

The Captain beamed. "You see how it works? This is merely a process that asks your mind for information it has already stored. Choose a word, a word closely related to your problem, and ask yourself what it reminds you of. Ask how you could use that word to solve your problem, and ideas will swim right to you. Now, you're well on your way and I must be too!"

The product development team gathered by the window to wave good-bye as the Captain punched the scaffold's down button and descended to another floor.

"Gee," Lenny said. "I could get to like this. OK, guys. Somebody suggest another word. I'll take over Ted's duties at the board. And remember, we're only looking for Word Bait to start."

"Clothing," someone shouted.

"Mittens"

"Gloves"

"Long johns"

"Long janes"

"Hey guys, we're talking about *summer* here."

Word Bait Lesson No. 1

The process of fishing for new concepts is just this simple: To come up with them, you only have to plumb your mind's depths and get the information that's already stored there. You do that by casting Word Bait into your mind's natural categories of stored information. Then, all of the associated concepts your mind has stored will swim back to you.

This process works according to the way the human mind organizes and remembers experiences; that is, by common associations, or links. Rather than store information—words—

alphabetically like a dictionary, or just by synonym like a thesaurus, the mind organizes information by association. That's why one concept leads you right to another.

Any piece of Word Bait is a direct link to your mind. By tossing a piece of Word Bait into one of your mind's categories of associations, you'll activate the process of Associational Thinking. The bait you toss in will prompt your mind to respond with other associated bait that is stored within the same category.

You've no doubt seen people who can remember the names of everyone in an audience. Remembering names demonstrates the principle of Associational Thinking just as flying a paper airplane across a family room demonstrates the principle of aerodynamics. In fact, it couldn't be done without thinking by association.

If you've ever played a free association game, you know that a given word will trigger multiple associations. For instance, if you cast the word driving into your mind, you might come up with speeding ticket, flat tire, and canyon road, all of which are associated in your mind with the concept of driving. But each also triggers a different concept about the subject of driving.

Now toss the Word Bait speeding ticket into your mind. What swims back? A personal experience? Too bad. Next, toss in flat tire. Personal experience again? Well then, change your thoughts once more by thinking about a canyon road. See? The Word Bait speeding ticket, flat tire, and canyon road have triggered three additional concepts in your mind about driving—concepts that can then be expressed in words.

From the Word Bait red, you may haul in Little Red Riding Hood, fire engine, valentine, sunset, or passion. They were "filed" under red and organized by your own associative relationships. That's why you can reconstruct your associations for red when that Word Bait is presented. Likewise, your mind can cross-reference. Red may make you think of valentine and valentine may make you think of red. And when comparing red with fire engine, you may get the associated images of danger, fear, and emergency. Yet when comparing red with valentine, you may come up with love, romance, and candy.

Since at any given time you can't remember all of the ideas you have stored, you need a way to maximize what you can remember. And that's what Word Bait does. It acts like a trigger to stimulate your memory. The more Word Bait you have, the more your memory and imagination will be triggered.

By definition, Word Bait is associated with the problem you're trying to solve. So when you begin to fill up your Bait Bucket, only evaluate the pieces on that basis. If a word isn't related, it isn't Word Bait. On the other hand, once you've hooked some real Word Bait, don't try to judge whether or not it's a keeper. That's of no importance at this stage. Instead, treat each piece as a valuable asset, a vital clue that could very well provide the link to your Big Catch.

And while you're fishing for more Word Bait, be sure to write down the pieces as they surface. It doesn't matter if you write them down on paper, on a chalk board, or on the inside of your wrist. But write them down. Otherwise they'll dart right back under that riverbank ledge you so carefully coaxed them from.

Without even thinking about it, idea anglers ask these two Word Bait Questions all the time.

1. What does this word make me think of?

2. How can I use this word—alone, some part of it, or in combination with another—to solve my problem?

Your answers to these questions are apt to be a little long. For instance, rather than just hook "hot town," you might pull aboard "hot in town." Throw back the little unimportant glue words such as *and*, *at*, *on*, other *prepositions*, *articles*, and *conjunctions* and keep filling up your Bait Bucket.

Throughout *The IdeaFisher*, you'll be learning a variety of ways to go angling for ideas, cast your bait, and even locate different fishing holes. For right now, start practicing the basics. Pick up your favorite cane pole, bait your hook, and toss your cork bobber into the Word Bait Exercise on page 43.

Hook, Line & Sinker

Now that you've seen an example of angling for new concepts in the short story and read the lesson, you might want to know how someone has applied the principle of Associational Thinking to solve actual problems or develop real ideas. You'll find these Hook, Line & Sinker excerpts throughout *The IdeaFisher*. Here's the first one about how a real life fisher followed the Captain's advice:

The initial Word Bait of paths and route set the Kobb Team of Houston, Texas, on a course for their new company slogan. "We do management development training and performance support," says Steve Kobb. "It's difficult to easily explain to others exactly what we do. But after fishing for just a few minutes we had our slogan, 'Creating pathways to your goals,' a logo concept of a pathway winding through mountain peaks, and several great concepts for our brochure."

Word Bait Exercise No. 1

Associational Thinking can be activated at will. And it's easy to learn how. Just try this simple exercise and see for yourself. Think about a car. Have you ever wished there was some way to make driving, or riding, more comfortable? Well, here's your chance.

The specific problem is: Create a new <u>comfort</u> feature for your <u>car</u>. And remember not to worry about technical feasibility—you just have to land that Big Idea.

Start by writing down on a sheet of paper your Word Bait for <u>comfort</u> and <u>car</u>. Then list all of the related words you can think of under each. Keep in mind that the more closely associated your Word Bait is to the problem, the sooner you'll have the solution!

For example:

Comfort	Car
air mattress	rear view mirror
backrest	windows
seat cover	steering wheel
throw pillow	brake

Go ahead. Take 15 minutes and fill up your own Bait Bucket. Next, apply the two Word Bait Questions to each word and write down your answers. Like this:

AIR MATTRESS:

1. What does this word make me think of?

   <u>inflate</u>

2. How can I use this word to solve my problem?

   make the <u>ride</u> feel like I'm <u>floating</u> <u>on</u> <u>air</u>

What about a **car seat cushion** that contains **air bladders** like an <u>air</u> <u>mattress</u> does? By simply adjusting it, anyone could drive in <u>comfort</u> all day!

Now, do the same with the other words on your list. If you run out of Word Bait, turn to Part Four: Fishing Tackle in the back of the book and you'll find Bait Buckets full of it.

F O U R

Berlin Wall:
Defining the Problem

"Monica, you must understand that this partnership agreement was written forty years ago. It clearly states that you and Ernst are equal partners, and there's no buyout provision. You'll have to negotiate a settlement with him, that is, if he's interested. In any event you most certainly cannot just fire him."

"Mein Gott!" shouted Monica, slamming down the phone. No attorney was going to tell Monica Tietze, the cofounder of Kuchen Kitchens International, what she could and could not do with Ernst Gude. She would do with Ernst Gude what she wanted, when she wanted, and as often as she wanted. After all, that's precisely what she had done since she was 16 years old.

*   *   *

Forty years ago, in Hamburg, Germany, Monica and Ernst had been teenage sweethearts. He had a natural talent for baking that everyone in the neighborhood knew about. In a country where virtually every other corner was filled with a bakery store, Ernst's apfelkuchen, sacher torts, and streusel were prized by the locals. Every evening he would prepare the sweet delicacies that Monica would sell door-to-door. By the time they were old enough to attend the University, Ernst and Monica had a thriving business along with a respectable savings account.

Then they had to make a decision: Should they open their own bakery shop, competing head-on with the several hundred shops already in the city, temporarily shut down the business and attend the University, or . . . ?

Monica had always wanted to live in the United States, the land of opportunity. Thanks to persistent urging on her part, Ernst finally agreed to move overseas for one year—just long enough to discover whether or not they could duplicate their hometown success in America.

Four decades later Kuchen Kitchens International had grown into a worldwide franchise of bakery shops, including two in Hamburg, and a chain of catering outlets with locations in every major metropolitan city of the United States. Unfortunately, the demands of a thriving business had caused Monica and Ernst's romantic relationship to fall by the wayside.

Midwife to the firm's prosperity, Monica oversaw every aspect of the business, save one. The recipes. Those were Ernst's domain. Having expanded his culinary capabilities into gourmet cuisine, he spent most of every day in his personal test kitchen.

Located adjacent to his office suite, Ernst's test kitchen was coveted by everyone who saw it. Monica had paid special attention to the kitchen's design, even accenting it with a wall of floor-to-ceiling windows overlooking the harbor, simply because that's where she wanted her partner to stay—in the kitchen and out of the business.

Nonetheless, roughly once a quarter she had to put out a fire Ernst would start in any one of the seven countries where the firm did business. He'd interrupt contract negotiations with a new franchisee in Belgium, order double inventories for a catering warehouse in Japan, halt construction on a new site in France, or, on a really bad day—call an emergency staff meeting just to discuss a new letterhead. Monica had quietly resorted to sending him on trips to research new recipes, while constantly outfitting his kitchen with an ever-changing array of new and expensive gadgets. As far as Monica was concerned, what had begun as bothersome interferences had turned into full-blown catastrophes. And what had begun as mutual love and admiration had finally turned into full-blown distrust and flat-out hatred.

This last go-around, the call from their friend and client Yolanda Baccus, the head of purchasing for Fairweather & Company, put Monica firmly over the edge. According to Yolanda, Ernst had offered to personally oversee catering for the groundbreaking ceremonies of Fairweather's new offices in Smithfield, but her guests were due in 45 minutes, there were no food trucks in sight, and she couldn't get ahold of him.

In quick succession, Monica made three phone calls. She reached the manager of the Kuchen Kitchen Katering outlet in Smithfield, who had never heard of Ms. Baccus but did have plenty of food and cakes on hand for her groundbreaking ceremony. He and his staff were commanded into action. Next, she called Yolanda back, apologized profusely, told her that a choice selection of delicious items was on its way, and waived the catering fee completely. And, then . . . Monica called her lead corporate attorney, the senior partner of Lynch, Cahn & Dodge, and got the worst news of her life.

As the phone slammed into its cradle, all of Monica's systems ratcheted to Red Alert. Her chafed nerve endings relayed their message. "Torpedo Room reporting. Veapon ready."

"Gut," came the reply.

A woman of Wagnerian stature, Monica Tietze strode out of her mahogany-paneled office in search of the quarry. The final countdown had begun. She crossed the executive secretaries' enclave, passed the huge inverted triangle shelves that held the firm's prestigious awards, and marched into enemy territory, where she would find her target.

Monica stormed into Ernst's executive suite and surveyed the area. He was not at his desk. She reached the door to his private kitchen, grabbed the knob, and yanked it open. There, next to the stove, stood Ernst, spoon in hand.

"Ya, Liebling?" he asked.

That was another thing she hated. He called anything with breasts Liebling.

Then, right between his baby blue Augen, she let him have it. The words roared out in rapid fire as she headed straight for Ernst with the possible intention of ramming him broadside. "Vas ist mit Yolanda? Du makes business trouble for last time! I close your office. Du have only kitchen for vork. No more mistakes. No more. Du are eine Katastrophe! Ist this, or I quit! I quit! No more, Ernst. Ist you or me. Vhich you vant? You tell me, Ernst, Du tell me, in eine hour—eine hour, Ernst, understand?"

Ernst dropped his spoon. A slight man who preferred "old country" styled clothing, Ernst looked toward the seething mass of rage, and timidly asked, "*Yolanda*?"

"Mein Gott! You idiot!" Working her neon yellow stilettos from the hips, Monica whirled about, gave it full throttle, and headed for open sea. Ernst watched the slamming door careen into its frame, bounce open, and come to its final rest against the floor, victim of a broken hinge.

The smell of burning turned Ernst's attention back to the stove. Gude's Gourmet Tartar Sauce, Version #1, had boiled its way free of confinement and run from the top of the stove to the top of Ernst's shoes. He studied the sauce's course, from point of origin to point of destination, while he wondered what Yolanda could ever have done to upset his partner so.

Monica decided to blow off steam by taking a walk along the quay. That would give Ernst his hour in which to decide whether or not to stay out of the business and in the kitchen, once and for all. She stood in front of the elevator, busy with her own thoughts, silently reaffirming the brilliance of her ultimatum.

"He never get out of this trap. He can't run business vithout me. He do as I say. He stay out of business und in kitchen or I quit und the company, the money, even test kitchen, vill all be gone. Vhy," she assured herself, "he don't know the company structure from a can of peas. Vhat vould he do vithout me? Just vhat vould he do vithout me?" Monica's coral lips spread into a smile she reserved for special occasions. "Vhy, he fall flat as soufflé," she concluded.

The elevator door jerked half-way open and then jerked forward to close again when Monica shoved a five-inch heel in its path. Pitching her formidable body sideways and exerting a single, great shove, she forced the door fully open. The elevator's temporary inhabitants stared at her.

"Ist nothing," said Monica, readjusting her jacket's shoulder pads.

*   *   *

As he walked into the Kuchen Kitchen offices, the Captain detected the scent of burnt Tartar Sauce, bringing him to the conclusion that Ernst was having a problem. He entered the co-owner's office and noticed the test kitchen's door ajar, one hinge hanging loose.

"Ernst, my friend, are you in some trouble?" he asked. Peering into the spacious galley, the Captain saw Ernst, wet dish cloth in hand, cleaning sauce from his shoelaces.

While they had both known the Captain for many years, Monica was the one who had spent the most time with him. Ernst had never so much as gotten to know the fellow's real name. "Nein, mein Captain," he responded with a shrug. "Ist only Monica. She ist angry again."

The Captain fully reviewed the scene with its broken door, messy stove, and ruined wing tips. "And what might have been the cause of this anger?"

Tartar-stained wash cloth in hand, Ernst pointed to a chair beside the art deco dining table, inviting his guest to sit down. "Oh, ist only something mit Yolanda Baccus. I know not vhat vas. Maybe bad vords."

"Bad words?" asked the Captain, sitting down. "From Yolanda? These words you refer to must have been potent indeed. The Yolanda Baccus I am acquainted with is a most unlikely source for such words. Should this be true, why is it Monica would take you to task for such a thing?"

"I know not," said Ernst sadly shaking his head. "Monica und me, ve have some problem, maybe."

"Well, my dear Ernst, prior to solving your problem, we must be certain that we are solving the *correct* one. In these instances, it's always best to begin with Defining the Problem Questions. Do you feel up to answering some questions in order to solve this problem?"

"Ya, sure," came the weary answer.

"What do you think Yolanda might have done to upset Monica so?"

"I know not."

"Well, what was the last item you and Yolanda spoke about?"

"Ein party for das office. Ein party. *Auch*!" Ernst slapped the side of his face with the dirty cloth. "Ein party for—for today! Das I have forget!"

"I assume you and Monica were to attend it."

"Nein, nein, ve vas to kater."

Feeling that perhaps this problem could be readily solved, the Captain's hazel eyes studied Ernst from across the ornate table. "Then this is what you forgot and what therefore caused today's exercise in target practice?"

"Vas no practice, mein Captain. Monica just say, she vant take my office avay und give me only kitchen for vork. She say I go from business or she go. In eine hour I tell her vas I do!"

Realizing now that defining this problem was going to take longer than expected, the Captain pulled a little notepad and pen from his shirt pocket. "My friend, an ultimatum is merely a reflection of a problem; it is not the problem itself. Perhaps we should continue."

"Ya, sure."

"Wonderful. Now then, what do you feel might occur should you simply ignore the problem?"

"Ist no one vhat ignore Monica, Captain," said Ernst.

"Quite right," responded the Captain. "When did the problem between you and Monica first appear?"

"America," said Ernst. "She vanted come, so ve came. She vanted run business, she run business. I cook. She go ein vay, I go ein other."

The Captain wrote down Ernst's answer and then asked, "What do you believe is the cause of this problem?"

"Ve no talk."

"Why has this problem continued unsolved?"

"Ve no speak long time, und so, ve no can speak. Ist something vas happens mit people."

"Ernst, by assuming that change is impossible, you therefore assume that nothing is possible. And not communicating isn't the problem. Merely a symptom of it." The Captain continued, "Do you really want to solve this problem? What if you simply left instead?"

"Auch, nein Captain! Monica, she ist all to me."

"What other things have changed in your relationship with Monica?"

Ernst looked around the kitchen. "In Germany," he answered, "ve go dancing, ve in love, ve vant to marry. But business, alvays business. So ve think later, maybe, later. But now ist too late."

"Look at this from Monica's point of view for a moment. What might she be thinking?"

"Ya, Ya. She hates me. I alvays in vay of business. Business she loves."

"Have you ever asked Monica about this?"

"Nein."

"What do you suppose you have done to add to this problem?"

"I cook, I travel, I not vith her much."

"Ernst, if this problem is not resolved, what is it you fear losing the most?"

"Oh . . . Monica!"

"And, what might occur should you attempt to speak with Monica about this apparent problem?"

He cast his eyes toward the ceiling and answered, "I know not."

"Might you possibly consider this current situation to be an opportunity to speak with her?"

Ernst looked down at the table, watching his finger draw circles on the polished granite. Finally, he said, "Maybe ve talk of this . . . und then, maybe ve talk of other things."

Allowing Ernst to begin to fully appreciate his own insights, the Captain quietly studied his notes for a moment, underlining the Word Bait:

business
no talk
Monica, all to me
dancing
love
marry
not with her

The Captain gently tapped the table with his fingers. "Well, I have an idea. What type of flower does Monica prefer above any other?"

"Magnolia."

Quickly writing in his notepad, the Captain said, "Then, my friend, I suggest you immediately go to the flower shop downstairs and get her a vase quite full of them." He tore out the page, handed it to Ernst and said, "Write this on the card. Mind you, it will not be the solution in and of itself, merely a step in the right direction."

Ernst read the note and smiled. "Ya, Captain! Now, I see vhat real problem ist!"

*   *   *

Monica worked her way back along the quay lined with fish stores and restaurants. She entered Cannery Village's courtyard and immediately spotted the Captain standing alongside the fountain.

"My dearest Monica," the Captain called out. "Might I have but a moment of your time?"

The Captain had given her considerable advice in the growth of Kuchen Kitchens; at the very least she owed him the courtesy of a response. "Ya, sure, Captain."

As she approached he added, "I understand that you and Ernst might wish some assistance in solving a problem."

Now just steps away, she asked, "Vhat, Captain?" In general, Monica had come to believe that her partner had the attention span of a ferret. For Ernst to discuss any situation with the Captain, he must have finally located some facsimile of a backbone. If nothing else, her lawyer would want to hear this.

He extended his hand in greeting. "What was it that I might assist you with?"

"Ya, Ya, Captain," conceded Monica, accepting his handshake. "Ve have problems always mit business."

"A few moments ago, Ernst allowed me to ask him some questions to help discover what the *real* problem is. We came to the conclusion that it isn't Yolanda's groundbreaking ceremony, it isn't his occasional straying into the company's business activities, and it isn't the ultimatum you gave him. In fact, we came to quite another realization altogether."

Monica was intrigued. "Ya?"

"Perhaps utilizing the same process, you and I might arrive at the very conclusion that Ernst and I did. Shall we give it a try?"

Curiosity was getting the best of her. She warily agreed.

So the Captain began to ask Monica some of the same questions he had asked Ernst. "If this problem should not be resolved, what is it you might lose?"

Having convinced herself that it could never happen, Monica mechanically answered, "Das company."

"Perhaps the added urgency to this matter might affect the quality of a decision. Might there be any goodness in delaying this impending confrontation?"

"Nein, Captain. Ist time now."

"Monica," urged the Captain, "what other problems might be associated with the present one?"

Hearing the sincerity in his voice, she looked up at him. "Ist forty years, mein Captain. Ist forty years too late."

"Monica," he said softly. "What is the worst thing that can happen should this problem not be resolved?"

The thought of Ernst surfaced immediately.

As if he had read her mind, the Captain softly said, "Monica, I feel perhaps the three of us have discovered the real problem. You and Ernst have simply **forgotten** you **love** one another."

"Ernst loves his kitchen," snapped Monica. "I must go now." She said a hasty good-bye and headed across the courtyard.

*   *   *

Monica entered her office and came to a full stop. There, atop her desk, sat a huge crystal vase filled with the biggest and most magnificent magnolias she had even seen. She gasped, and hurried over to them. There was an envelope. It was addressed to Miss Tietze. She plucked it out and opened it. The card inside read, "Monica, would you be so kind to attend the dance with me on Saturday?" It was signed, "Love, Ernst."

"Ya, liebling?" came the timid voice from behind her. Monica's eyes began to fill with tears. She turned and saw Ernst—in his stocking feet.

"Ya, liebling!"

Word Bait Lesson No. 2

It's amazing how many people go about trying to solve a problem without first clarifying exactly what the problem is. Sure, they have some idea about it, in a broad, general way. Perhaps they want to come up with a new packaging design, solve world hunger, write a book, or get into the film business.

Usually, they try to solve the problem like this:

"I'll just think about it and figure it out."

"I know! I'll bounce this off some of my friends."

"Maybe a walk on the beach would help."

They then proceed to think-think-think, hold a meeting, or put the project off until next year. Sound familiar? Or, how about this? When trying to solve a problem, do you doodle? Pace around? Gaze at the ceiling, or even a little higher for divine guidance? Clench your fists? Your teeth? How far does any of that really get you?

The truth of the matter is that until you specifically define your problem, both you *and* your pencil will be going around in circles.

To define a problem, you need to ask yourself some specific questions . . . Defining the Problem Questions. That's how the Captain helped Ernst and Monica. By asking questions, he forced them to clarify the real problem . . . not just its symptoms.

Clearly defining your problem is a matter of zeroing in on the heart of it, progressively narrowing your focus until you have pared it down into manageable proportions. The more nebulous a problem seems, the more critical this step is.

Say you want to write a book. Good! What kind of book? Is it going to be fiction, nonfiction, biography, autobiography, textbook, or poetry? Will it be set in the past, present, or future? Does it deal with business, science, health, cooking, travel, art, or the circus? The more clearly you can state the problem, the better.

For another example, suppose you want to create a new packaging design. You could spend a great deal of time thinking about all kinds of designs. You could travel the world studying different packaging designs and still arrive home without any answers, just because you haven't defined the problem.

You need to be more specific. So, what if you changed the problem from "new packaging design" to "new packaging design for food?" Better get your frequent flyer vouchers out . . . it'll be another long trip. How about new packaging design for tacos? Well, would it be for fish, chicken, or beef tacos? The design would differ dramatically for each.

If you reply "new packaging design for fish tacos," you've clearly established what the problem is simply by answering questions that narrowed your focus. And look how these questions have changed the words packaging and design into real Word Bait!

Hook, Line & Sinker

See how the right questions helped an entrepreneur expand his business:

Rick Raymond teaches at New York University and is the president of his own environmental consulting company, Richard Raymond Associates, Inc., in New York City. He wanted to develop a new training program, but what type? By working with Defining the Problem Questions Rick created the new workshop, "Corporate Environmental Awareness Training." "The questions helped me prepare a two-page synopsis and a five-page description of the workshop; in essence a business plan without the numbers attached," says Rick.

Word Bait Exercise No. 2

The most difficult part of solving a problem is often *how* to begin solving it. Defining the Problem Questions will serve as icebreakers, helping you see just where to begin.

Sometimes you won't know what the actual problem is until you see its solution. Other times, midway, you'll discover you should have taken a different track. But you obviously must start somewhere, and the following Defining the Problem Questions are designed for just that purpose.

Think about a problem you're currently trying to solve. Perhaps you need to develop a new product, discover additional applications for an existing product, create a packaging design, generate variations on a story theme, seek a scientific breakthrough, troubleshoot a problem, invent a process, design a new machine, or plan an advertising campaign. To clearly define your problem, read through the following questions. Take 30 minutes to jot down your answers on a piece of paper—your Bait Bucket. You needn't try to answer all the questions, because each one doesn't apply to the same type of problem. After the first question (it's the most important for everyone), you should choose only those that directly apply. Underline the Word Bait in your answers and spend another 15 minutes fishing for your Catch—the solution to your problem.

1. What are you trying to accomplish? Consider:

   What is the problem? What is the challenge?

   What must be decided?

2. What if you were simply to ignore the situation? Might time alone solve the problem?

3. If it won't go away by itself, is the problem really worth solving?

   Who agrees that this is an important challenge, and why?

   Which relevant persons regard it as unimportant, and why?

   By solving the problem, what do you stand to gain?

   What do others stand to lose?

What is the worst that can happen if the problem is not resolved?

4. What resources can you dedicate to reaching a solution?

5. How should decisions along the way to a solution be reached?

   Who should be involved in arriving at decisions?

   Who should make the final decision?

   In what manner should decisions be made (such as unilaterally, by majority vote, by consensus)?

6. How will you know when you have achieved your purpose? What are your criteria for success? For example:

   What will people be doing well? How will they feel about their work? How will they be getting along with each other?

   How will your own work be easier or more enjoyable? What will you no longer have to attend to? What will you no longer be concerned about?

7. Regarding your own interest in the matter, what are your personal and professional reasons for working on this project?

   What risks or threats must you face in solving this problem?

   What is most fearsome or threatening about the problem itself?

8. How strong is your personal commitment to the effort? Are you willing to invest the necessary time and energy?

   Might you be overstimulated or too motivated to reach a conclusion? How might this urgency affect the quality or ethics of your decision?

9. Whose problem is it?

   Is it really your problem? What if you transfer responsibility?

10. When was the need or trouble first noticed? Did it occur suddenly, or had it been developing for some time before anyone noticed it?

    How did it manifest itself? What were the symptoms or indicators that something needed attention?

11. How did you become aware of the situation?

    When did you become aware of it? How do you feel about the timing, or about the way you were informed?

    What else do you know about the history of the problem?

12. What do you now understand about the cause or causes of the problem?

13. Why hasn't the problem already been solved?

14. What is the crux of the issue? To gain other perspectives so you don't solve the wrong problem:

    Who can give you a different perspective on the nature of the problem and the crux of the issue?

    Whose point of view should be considered because the person is directly affected by the problem?

    What if you also get the perspective of at least one person who appreciates the problem but who is not directly affected by it?

    What if you make believe that you are several different people, viewing the same set of facts from various perspectives (with different vested interests)?

15. What do you believe is the extent of the problem? (How pervasive or widespread is it? What is its magnitude in numbers?)

    How quickly is the problem spreading or developing? What is the risk of time passing without resolution?

    What if you seek a temporary solution before a permanent one?

    Who can give you an unbiased perspective on the magnitude or seriousness of the problem? (Perhaps someone who has faced a similar challenge, or someone outside your domain.)

16. How complex is the problem? What other problems are linked with this one? How are they interrelated? For example:

    How does one problem lead to—or result from—another?

    What small problems add up to this big problem or make it worse?

17. If you're not fully aware of the assumptions guiding your work, why continue wearing blinders? Consider:

    Are you aiming at the right target? Are you working on the right problem?

    Have you oversimplified the problem?

    What are you taking for granted about the urgency of a solution? What if you just wait and see what happens?

    What do you assume are the givens that can't be changed? What if you change them anyway?

    What are you assuming to be impossible? What if you try it nevertheless?

What procedures do you assume are necessary? What if you skip them?

What "facts" have you assumed to be correct: How might the information fool you?

What trouble can you redefine as an opportunity?

18. Have any of your answers to these questions changed your thinking about the subject?

    How has the challenge grown or expanded? What does it now encompass?

    Do you now see it as one problem, or as several interrelated problems or sub-problems?

    What do you now think is the root cause of the problem, or what causes appear to be intermeshed?

    What do you now believe is the crux of the issue?

    Whose problem is it now? If it's not yours now, why stay involved?

    Considering the big picture, what about this problem is most important?

    What is the most difficult barrier to a satisfying solution?

    What is now your primary aim/goal/objective?

    What about the problem is most urgent, or most in need of immediate attention?

19. How do these changes in your thinking affect the decisions that must be made?

    How do the changes in your thinking affect the manner in which decisions should be reached?

20. How confident are you that you have framed the central problem, rather than a side issue or a false problem? (What is your level of confidence, such as "95 percent sure"?)

    How likely is it that the real problem will not be known until you have reached at least a partial solution?

21. What are your thoughts about a final deadline for reaching a satisfying conclusion?

22. Did your definition of the problem drastically change? If so, return to the beginning of these questions and answer them again with your new perspective in mind.

23. Who else is engaged in trying to solve this problem?

    Who else should be involved? (What other groups, agencies, and individuals share your interest? Why should they participate?)

    How can you enlist their participation?

    Who is involved but should not be? Why is their participation not relevant or not helpful?

    Are any who are trying to solve this problem actually making it worse? (In what way? What happens?)

    How can you change the efforts that are not appropriate or not helpful (as by remedial instruction, reassignment, removal from the project, or asking the people what they think)?

24. Whose attitude or behavior is the problem or part of the problem?

    What have other people done to perpetuate the situation? (Who has done what, or failed to do what, and for what reason?)

What have you done to perpetuate the situation?

25. Who has a vested interest in the status quo? How do they benefit from things as they are—and what do they think they'll lose if the problem is solved?

    Are those with a vested interest actually part of the problem?

    How likely is it that those with a vested interest will resist your efforts? What form might their resistance take?

    What thought have you given to coping with the self-protective behavior of those who wish to maintain the status quo?

    What thought have you given to mutual problem solving?

26. If the issue involves conflict between personal value systems, how are emotions interfering with efforts to find a solution?

27. What other emotions are interfering? For example:

    What negative emotions—such as anger, envy, resentment, mistrust, wounded pride, or protection of territory/turf—are affecting the attitudes of those whose help you need?

    How are the feelings expressed in people's behavior?

    What positive attitudes might also be interfering (such as conscientiousness or extreme loyalty to company/colleagues)?

    How are the attitudes expressed in people's behavior?

    How important is it to deal with the positive and negative feelings before you forge ahead? What thought have you given to the way this might be done?

28. If this is primarily a "people problem," or if someone's "misconduct" is of central concern, what is the nature of the behavior, and who is engaged in it?

    To whom is the behavior objectionable, and for what reason?

    What appears to be the purpose of the "misconduct"? (To gain attention? To win a power struggle? To seek revenge?)

    To check your analysis: How does the recipient of this behavior feel when the person behaves this way? (Irritated? Challenged? Defeated? Hurt?)

    What other payoffs does the "perpetrator" gain from this behavior?

    What do you think the person is trying to say about himself or herself by engaging in this conduct (such as I'm powerful . . . I'm brave . . . I'm smarter than you . . . I'm important . . . I need help)?

29. Who else do you think may be contributing to the behavior by egging it on or approving of it?

    What satisfaction or reward do those in the background gain by tolerating or contributing to the "misconduct"?

30. What efforts have been made to stop or modify the behavior? (Who has done what with whom?)

    How does the person respond to your efforts to stop the behavior?

    What happens when you steadfastly ignore it?

    What happens when you allow logical consequences to take their course (such as allowing the person to experience failure, rather than rescuing or covering for the person)?

As a quick reference guide for your convenience, a listing of these task-specific questions, along with those from other chapters of *The IdeaFisher*, is included in Part 4: Fishing Tackle.

Hook, Line & Sinker

Some folks go fishing for lots of reasons:

When they needed to select a new Musical Director, Pastor Graeme Rosenau of Mount Olive Lutheran Church in La Mirada, California, went angling before presenting the problem to his special committee. According to Pastor Rosenau, "By going through the Defining the Problem Questions, I was able to develop a concise new job description that the committee considered a major improvement over the old one." The pastor also uses this process to develop ideas for sermons, articles, classes, and retreats.

F I V E

For Hire:
The Six Universal
Questions

Thursday Night

Dear Mom,

    Well, the good news first. I have another
interview set for tomorrow at 9:00 a.m.!! (Now the
bad news.) This week was a bust. What I don't
understand is why people would invite me to come
in and be interviewed if the last thing they want
is another "MBA fresh from college with no
practical experience." I'm beginning to think I'm
just fodder for honing interview skills. And the
employment agencies are a joke. They expect me to
pay them up front with no guarantee that they'll
find me a job!! I may not have much practical
business experience, but I know a dumb deal when I
see one.

    Don't tell Susie, but it looks as if this
grand plan of mine isn't going to work. It's been
one month and not so much as a real job offer.
Harry's been great putting me up so long. You'll
be amazed at how good a dishwasher I've become! I
help with expenses as much as I can, but with no

income I'll be lucky to make it another 30 days. (THIS IS NOT A PLEA FOR MONEY SO PLEASE DON'T SEND ANY.)

I guess what I'm really saying is don't be surprised if I come home, professionally printed Joshua Filipack résumés in hand, and take that position at the electric company. If it's still open. Deadly dull or not, it would be enough to put beans on the table, a roof over my head, and in time, a down payment on Susie's engagement ring.

Harry just walked in from the kitchen (his turn to play Julia Child). He wanted to say Hi! to you and alert me that the Ketchup is missing. I asked him if they took anything else. Now he's headed for the Parmesan's last known location. Film at eleven . . .

Ah, well, what is it Grandpa used to say? "Any experience you learn from is a good experience?" So far I've learned about all the mistakes (I hope there aren't more) I've made to date. When you feel stupid it's hard to look smart.

Well, wish me luck!!

Love You A Bunch!

Josh

P.S. Julia just informed me that the Spaghetti Surprise is ready.

Friday ■ 9:46 a.m.

The elevator doors slammed open and Josh stumbled out. Moving through the courtyard on automatic pilot, he didn't see the scurrying seagulls, smell the fresh saltwater, hear the sailboat halyards bouncing against their masts, or notice the fellow in white walking lockstep beside him.

"This isn't going to work," he said to himself. "*Who* do these people think they are? *What's* the point? *Why* do I keep putting myself through this?"

"I should say that three out of six of the questions is an excellent start," responded the Captain.

Hearing the voice behind him, Josh's senses kicked into high gear. "Excuse me? Oh, nuts! I was talking out loud. I mean thinking . . . I mean . . . For crying out loud, you must think I'm crazy!"

"Not at all, Josh," assured the Captain. "By the way, you passed me on the fourth floor and dropped a few of your résumés. I thought you might not mind, so I glanced at them in the elevator."

Josh turned and took his first full-length look at the Captain: Sporting a reddish beard and a pair of bifocals that slipped to the end of his nose when he looked down, he was wearing a painter's uniform, deck shoes, and a set of garish suspenders.

"I passed you? That's funny, I don't remember seeing you."

"Perhaps you were preoccupied. It isn't hard to see that your job interview at the Great Outdoors Apparel Company was not a resounding success."

Sensing that the Captain's concern was genuine, Josh responded, "It was a waste of time. Turns out they hired somebody last week. The least they could have done was to call me to cancel the appointment."

"So my friend, what's next on your agenda? Another interview?"

"Not today, and I've already read the want ads. Guess I'll go back to Harry's and keep trying to figure out how to get a decent job in this town. Or, maybe I'll pack my bags for home."

"There is no room for remorse in a suitcase, Josh. Why don't you join me for a cup of coffee instead?" The Captain pointed toward The Catch espresso cafe. "Perhaps we'll fish around for some new job possibilities for you."

Thinking his day was shot anyhow, Josh answered, "*What's* to lose?"

"*What* is an excellent place to start; however, it's only one of the six questions," noted the Captain as they entered the cozy restaurant. "You will understand what I'm talking about in a moment. First, however, I should properly introduce myself. Most people call me Captain. I've known this place since it was a fish cannery. Now I perform odd jobs such as, well, such as washing windows so that people might gain a clearer perspective on things."

A smiling hostess greeted them. "Your table is ready, Captain."

"Thank you, my dear Sylvie. Coffee for two, please." The Captain and Josh crossed the oak plank floor, heading for the window table that offered the most expansive view of the bay.

Cannery Village was situated atop a spit of land that jutted into the harbor. Off to the left, deep-sea trawlers, heavy with the morning's catch, moved slowly toward their slips. A knot of Sabot sail boats, filled with a novice apiece, haltingly edged its way into the wind off to the right. Soft gusting breezes brought with them the sounds of children laughing as they tried to round the first race buoy. Slowed by the legal five-knot limit, oceangoing speed boats with tanks full of testosterone, announced their passing as emphatically as impatient gladiators about to enter the ring. And all the while, stately yawls held silent dockside vigil.

Born and raised in landlocked mid-state, Josh found himself fascinated with the coast. "This would be a heck of a place to work," he commented, loosening his "power tie."

"Which is precisely why I invited you for coffee," responded the Captain as they settled into the rich wood and leather deck chairs. He reached into his shirt pocket and pulled out the little notepad complete with glistening pen anchored in its spiral. Sylvie arrived with the coffee service and arranged two Bernardou china cup and saucer sets on the mauve linen tablecloth.

Seeing the notepad, Sylvie asked, "First fishing trip?" Josh's puzzled look confirmed her suspicion. Nodding in the Captain's direction she added, "Trust me, he's more than he appears to be. If it weren't for him, I wouldn't have been able to buy The Catch. By the way, Captain, the contract negotiations should be complete in the next few weeks."

"That is marvelous news, Sylvie," said the Captain, setting down his cup of rich Kona coffee. "I'm delighted to hear it. Josh, this is one of my dear friends, Sylvie Simonait, who is about to go into business for herself. Sylvie, I'd like you to meet my new friend, Joshua Filipack.''

"You mean you invested money in the restaurant?''

Raising a brow in surprise, Sylvie replied, "Oh, no! Nothing *that* simple. He helped me come up with a lot of new ideas and I took it from there.'' As she left to wait on her other guests, Sylvie said, "Believe me, Josh, the Captain's principles can navigate you through any rough waters.''

The young MBA looked at his host. "New ideas, huh? I could use a few of those.''

"I realize this might be difficult for you to believe, Josh, but you already have all the ideas you need, tucked away in your mind. Our job is to bring them to the surface.'' Noticing his skeptical look, the Captain chuckled and began to tell Josh about the concept of angling for new ideas with Word Bait.

Some moments later he concluded his explanation by adding, "In a way you're lucky, Josh. Your problem is already clearly defined: finding a job. What you need now are some bright shiny lures to attract the really good Word Bait. One of the best ways to attract concepts that are associated with your problem is to simply answer some questions—using the questions as lures. Even though the number of questions that may be asked about any problem is infinite, it's easiest to start off with the Six Universal Questions that everyone can remember: *Who, what, where, when, why,* and *how.* I call them the six-hook lure. We'll attach your initial Word Bait, finding a job, to the lure by simply keeping finding and job in mind as you answer the questions. Your answers will be full of even bigger Word Bait that we will use to haul in your Catch.'' The Captain opened up his notepad. "Shall we give it a try?''

"Sure."

"*Who* do you know in town?"

"Just Harry, my best friend from the fifth grade, who is putting me up for awhile. Oh, and of course you . . . and, now, I guess Sylvie, as well." The Captain wrote Josh's answer in his notepad.

"*What* could Harry do to help you get a job?"

"Not much. He just got laid off so he's pretty busy trying to work his own contacts for job leads. I can understand why he doesn't want to share them with me just yet."

"*What* is your hometown?"

"Smithfield."

"*What* could you do to overcome your lack of work experience?"

"Work for free—no one seems to want to pay me."

"Negativity doesn't belong in any fishing expedition," corrected the Captain.

"Sorry."

"*Where* could you go to show off your capabilities?"

"Renting a booth at a trade show is about the dumbest idea I can think of."

"Judgment does not belong in a fishing expedition either," corrected the Captain again.

"Sorry again."

"*When* is the last day you must decide whether or not to return home?"

"Probably within 30 days or so."

"*Why* do you want to work here rather than your home town? Smithfield is midway between two of the state's biggest cities, and I understand it is growing rapidly."

"There's lots of new office buildings being built; in fact, they're overbuilding, which makes the office space cheap. So Smithfield is attracting new businesses, but they're corporations that have recently downsized; they already have all the staff they need."

"*What* type of engineering is your degree in?"

"Mechanical engineering. Pumps and valves. That type of thing."

"*How* could a variety of people from a variety of companies see your potential all at once?"

"Oh, I don't know. Maybe some sort of a talent showcase like singing groups have."

"*What* do you feel your strongest abilities are?"

"Definitely organizational: detail work, dotting *i*'s, crossing *t*'s, that type of thing. In fact, the more things I have to organize the better. I'm a self-starter."

"*How* did Harry go about initially finding a job in town?"

"During his junior year of college he started going around to various companies here, getting acquainted with them and expressing his interest in working for them after he graduated.

Pretty clever actually. He got to know lots of people and wound up with a number of job offers by the time he got his degree."

"*What* type of industry would you prefer to work in?"

"Just about any. I really don't know."

"Josh, you must answer the questions directly and thoroughly. It is best not to avoid them with an 'I don't know,' " the Captain admonished.

"Well, looking back, I think the only reason I picked engineering was because of my sense of organization. It was a way to get through college. Not something I enjoy doing per se. I've always sort of had an interest in finance, being good with numbers and such." Josh hesitated. "Captain? Not to be rude or anything, but I don't really see where this Spanish Inquisition is getting us."

"A number of people say that very thing at first. Trust me, Josh, serious fishing, just like any endeavor, requires dedication, time, and practice."

"Okay. Resume course."

"*Where* have you worked before?"

"Smithfield isn't much of a town, and a summer job, if you can find one, is pretty boring fare. I've worked as a counter clerk at a copier shop, delivery person for a local florist, kitchen help for a catering service, and some construction work with Harry."

"*How* have you gone about looking for a job up until now?"

"The usual stuff. Looking at the classifieds in the newspaper, sending out résumés, going on interviews. I even checked out employment agencies but that was a waste of time."

The Captain reviewed his notes. "This is delightful. It looks as if our six-hook lure is more than full. There should be enough here to start fishing for even bigger Word Bait. Shall we see what we have?" With that, the Captain began to review his transcript of Josh's answers, underlining a word or two in each, and creating a fresh list of Word Bait. The result was:

contacts
share
work for free
trade show
talent showcase
organize
self-starter
handyman

Looking at Josh from over the rims of his bifocals, the Captain asked, "Keeping your problem of finding a job in mind, what do these words make you think of?"

Josh's frown announced his feelings. "They make me think I'm sunk!"

At that, the Captain separated a few sheets from his notepad, handing them and a pencil to Josh. "Shall we do some fishing together? I believe you will be pleasantly surprised."

Working together, the two of them found that contacts led to networking and groups of people. Share expanded to sharing time and talent. Work for free gave way to charity and nonprofit organization. Trade show developed into trading volunteer work for work experience and references. Talent showcase became group effort. Organize was transformed into organizations. And, self-starter changed into volunteer. Lastly, handyman brought up the concept of offering to do anything.

Contemplating work for free, Josh leaned back in the deck chair and held his pencil with both hands as if it were a rod poised to strike a prized Marlin. His thoughts began to play from one idea to the next. The 100-pound line tugged just slightly—once, twice. His eyes narrowed. He clasped the pencil tighter. And just then the line came to life, smoking and bending the rod as it spun out faster and faster. He'd hooked the idea good and deep and Josh instantly released the reel break. His catch raced for the surface. It was running for air, about to break out of the water when Josh slammed the rod down on the table and proclaimed, "I got it, I got it! This is a great idea. It's dynamite!"

Quickly reaching to steady the bouncing coffee cups, the Captain urged, "Perhaps we should take a look at what you brought in before it tips us overboard."

"I'll **volunteer** for a **local charity**! You know, work for free. That way lots of people will see me in action. It'd be a real showcase for my talents and I'll make plenty of contacts!" Josh was ecstatic.

"Excellent!" said the Captain. "I believe you will find information regarding a number of charities in the local newspaper."

"I'll take another look at it right away!"

Friday Night

Dear Susie,

What a day! My interview this morning was a waste of time, except for this amazing guy I met.

Everybody calls him the Captain and he really
helped me with this job thing just by asking some
questions, and, well, really it's all about
fishing for new concepts. You see . . .

Word Bait Lesson No. 3

So now you know how to clearly define your problem, how to use little pieces of Word Bait from your Bait Bucket to attract even larger Word Bait, and how to use that to reel in your Big Idea, a Catch that may be good enough to put in your Idea Creel.

Is that all there is to it?

Nope.

Occasionally, fishing does go that smoothly. But more often than not, you'll need some way to nudge yourself into deeper, more productive, waters. In order to consistently reel in a Catch worthy of your Idea Creel, you need to put your Word Bait on the right lures. Asking questions is the best way to do that. It's the way you've gotten information all your life.

Have you ever noticed that when someone asks you a question, your instinctive impulse is to answer it? Except by sheer force of will, and even that feels artificial, you can't avoid answering it.

When you ask *yourself* a question, you are forcing your mind to focus on a specific concern. Rather than aimlessly wandering around, it zeroes in on one thought.

While fishing for new concepts just think of every question as a lure, a hook, to which you attach your initial Word Bait. The more closely associated to the problem those questions are, the deeper your Word Bait will swim.

For a starting point, you may want to use the Six Universal Questions: *Who, what, where, when, why,* and *how.* These aren't just questions that journalists, scientists, and members of your local police department ask. The basis of most any question, they're easy to remember and readily serve as a way to attract bigger Word Bait. Each of them can be used as the first word of a question that is closely associated with your particular dilemma, whether it be finding a job or resolving a social problem. Here's an example to show you how.

Some years back, a national grocery store chain cornered the market on bananas. Hal, the president of produce, had the job of selling those bananas. He knew his problem. *Where* did he start to fish for a solution? Right in his office as usual! And here's the very list of questions that he asked himself:

1. He asked some *who* questions:

    Who will buy the bananas?

    Who will prepare the bananas for display?

    Who grows the bananas?

2. He asked some *what* questions:

    What is the price of the bananas?

    What benefits do the bananas produce?

    What promotions on fruit have we done in the past?

3. He asked some *where* questions:

Where will people buy the bananas?

Where will people hear about the bananas?

Where will we display the bananas?

4. He asked some *when* questions:

   When is the first shipment of bananas due in?

   When will the bananas be too old for sale?

   When can people buy the bananas?

5. He asked some *why* questions:

   Why would someone buy bananas?

   Why do people need bananas?

   Why are bananas yellow?

6. He asked some *how* questions:

   How will people purchase the bananas?

   How will people prepare the bananas?

   How are the bananas being shipped?

The prez answered the Six Universal Questions on the banana dilemma, underlining his Word Bait like this:

1. *Who* will prepare the bananas for display?

   The store clerks.

2. *What* promotions on fruit have we done in the past?

   We held an apple pie contest last year.

3. *Where* will we put the bananas?

   In the produce section and maybe by the front door.

4. *When* can people buy the bananas?

During <u>store</u> <u>hours</u> of 9:00 a.m. to 9:00 p.m.

5. *Why* would someone buy bananas?

Because they're <u>healthy</u>.

6. *How* will people purchase bananas?

With their <u>money</u>.

Knowing he could do even better if he used each of the minnows to attract bigger Word Bait, Hal went looking for deeper water.

> Minnow—<u>store</u> <u>clerks</u>
>> bigger Word Bait—<u>all</u> <u>ages</u>
>>> <u>helpful</u>
>>> <u>uniform</u>
>>> <u>check-out</u> <u>register</u>

> Minnow—<u>contest</u>
>> bigger Word Bait—<u>kids</u>
>>> <u>bake-off</u>
>>> <u>store-sales</u>

> Minnow—<u>front</u> door
>> bigger Word Bait—<u>back</u> <u>door/loading</u> <u>dock</u>
>>> in the <u>aisles</u>
>>> at the <u>check</u> <u>stand</u>

> Minnow—<u>store</u> <u>hours</u>
>> bigger Word Bait—<u>before/after</u> <u>hours</u>

> Minnow—<u>healthy</u>
>> bigger Word Bait—<u>nutritionist</u>
>>> <u>vitamins</u>
>>> <u>minerals</u>

> Minnow—<u>money</u>
> bigger Word Bait—<u>coupons</u>
> <u>script</u>
> <u>rebate</u>

Here are the Big Ideas that Hal hauled in:

1. <u>Uniform</u>—Sales **clerks** wearing **banana costumes**.

2. <u>Kids</u>—A **fund drive** tied in with **local schools**? Hold an on-site banana **costume contest** for the kids. A "**Bananarama**" with the winner being named the "**Top Banana**."

3. In the <u>aisles</u>—Banana **discount coupons** next to every food item in the store that would go with bananas, e.g., Jell-O.

4. <u>Before/after hours</u>—An on-site "**Banana Breakfast Blowout**," same concept as a pancake breakfast for a local charity.

5. <u>Nutritionist</u>—Tie in with a local **hospital**. Promote healthy eating with the hospital nutritionist providing recipes to give away at the hospital and the store. **Joint advertising**.

6. <u>Script</u>—Buying "x" amount of bananas at once entitles the customer to a **cash discount** of some amount on their next trip to the store.

Working with his Regional Managers, Hal fine-tuned the campaigns and put them in place across the country over a thirty-day period. As you can imagine, the grocery chain sold bananas by the zillions. And Hal? He's now one of the highest-paid grocery consultants in the country.

Hook, Line & Sinker

The Great American Novel in the making:

Mike Bartman of Potomac, Maryland, wanted to write a short story around the concept of "a spell caster in the Army." He hooked his initial Word Bait to a *"What"* question: *"What* type of world would this spell caster live in?" Mike pulled in the bigger Word Bait of magic. Fishing through all of the associations with magic, he was able to develop wondrous new spells and names of objects to populate his new world where magic worked like science.

Word Bait Exercise No. 3

Dick and Jane go to school. Dick and Jane buy drugs at school. Dick and Jane are 10 years old.

You are the principal of Dick and Jane's school.

You have a problem.

Now it's your turn. You know the problem: Drugs are being sold on the school grounds. It's time to haul out your "tackle box," rummage around for that six-hook lure, and go to work.

Get a piece of paper and bait your Six Universal Question hooks with: drugs, sold, and school grounds. Give yourself 15 minutes to write down the questions. Then give yourself another 15 minutes to answer them. With the last 15 minutes, go fishing for concepts to solve your problem.

Hook, Line & Sinker

See how just one question made all the difference:

By answering just one of the Six Universal Questions, "*What* do you like to do?," architect Marsden Moran of New Orleans, Louisiana, was able to decide whether or not to go into business for himself. The answer to that question enabled him to realize that there were three facets about his industry that he liked to do: schematic design, design development, and contract administration. He also discovered that there were two elements he'd rather not deal with: working drawings and bidding/negotiations. Since then, he has officially opened his design firm, Marsden Leverich Moran, Architect, and does only the things he loves to. He's developed a partnership with another architectural firm to provide for working drawings and bidding/negotiations. Marsden also used the Six Universal Questions to help his church develop a mission statement and to rename a hotel he remodeled.

S I X

Seeing 50:
Visualization

Wrapped in a ship's blanket, Claudia yanked open the door to her suite, stepped into the hallway, and was instantly greeted by darkness and a dead quiet. Sound sleeper or not, how could she possibly have missed an evacuation of the ship? There must have been plenty of noise, commotion, and confusion in emptying the cruise liner. She pulled the blanket tighter around her.

Looking toward the top of the companionway, she spotted the wine sommelier who had served them at the Captain's table earlier that evening. He began to wave frantically, calling to her in Italian. What a time to leave my Italian/English dictionary home she thought, as she began to climb the stairway.

Thankful for assistance, she followed the sommelier to the salon. When its double doors opened she saw a small circle of light bright enough for a Fiji sunset. Then, suddenly the entire room lit up and she saw Ian, still in the King Neptune outfit he'd worn for the evening's talent show, standing above a fully lit birthday cake. The voices of hidden guests joined in raucous chorus and began to sing "Happy Birth—"

In shock, Claudia released the ship's blanket that encircled her.

And Claudia Tochelle faced the guests of her surprise fiftieth birthday party in her birthday suit.

*   *   *

"Claudia! Claudia! Wake up. Are you all right?"

The birthday girl raised her head toward the voice, opened her eyes, and looked at her Aunt Ginna. "You were shouting in your sleep so loudly I thought it best to wake you. Are you all right?" she repeated. "It must have been a horrible nightmare the way you were shouting."

Shaking her head, Claudia began to recall her dream and the stunned look on her boyfriend's face as her blanket followed Newton's law straight to the floor. She made a mental note to tell Ian that's not a look Federal Regulators liked to see on a bank president's face. It makes them nervous.

"Not to worry, kiddo," Claudia answered, laughing a little as she struggled to free herself of the bed sheet. "Just a good old case of the 'turning fifty jitters.' Looking at her watch, she added, "It's six o'clock. We'd better get going."

*   *   *

Having seen her Aunt safely board the train, Claudia turned her car west, heading for the harbor, Cannery Village, and her office. Thirty minutes later, the CEO of Tochelle Travel, Inc., walked into the courtyard. Sounds of splashing water captured her attention, bringing her thoughts to a halt as she looked at the huge fountain. If set free from his mooring, Neptune looked as if he'd run over anyone . . . on sea *or* land. Especially with those—let's see, one, two, three, four—that figures, five dolphins under foot.

Remembering the dream, Claudia began to grin and shake her head. God or no God, she thought, you won't give me a surprise fiftieth birthday party.

As usual, her staff had gathered in Claudia's corner office for the Monday morning management meeting. Riccardo from finance was standing by the window watching two sea lions in the harbor below play what appeared to be the aquatic equivalent of tag alongside a slow charter boat of tourists. Head of sales Saul Overend was already seated at the circular glass conference table reviewing next month's projections, while the office manager, Beryl Whitcomb, and Francis Guerro, Claudia's assistant, sat shoulder to shoulder reading the front page of the morning newspaper.

"The term 'harvesting' is such a silly euphemism. Why don't they just come out and say they're going to kill hundreds of sea lions because the pleasure boaters and local fishermen don't like them?" asked Beryl.

"Because that would get people angry. And angry people are apt to take action," responded Francis. "I'll tell you who's really going to get angry—Claudia."

As if on cue, the agency's CEO stepped into her office. "Do tell," she said encouragingly, "What's Claudia really going to get angry about?"

"Listen to this," said Beryl, as she started to read the *Daily Record* article aloud. When she'd finished, Claudia, the resident environmentalist, spoke up first.

"That's crazy! Those seals were here long before any Chris Craft crossed the harbor or any fisher monger dropped a net."

"Somebody ought to do something," said Francis, knowing full well the response he was about to get.

"You bet. And we will," said his boss. Tossing the morning's agenda aside, Tochelle Travel's top management group set about developing a plan that would "S.O.S."—Save Our Seals.

"I'll call the University's Marine Biology Center to see what can be done to spare these guys from Harpoon Harry," announced Beryl.

"Whatever can be done will take money," said Riccardo.

Beryl offered to "pass the hat" among the office staff. Claudia noted that it would take a good bit more than that. "But with the contacts our Corporate Division has, we should be able to shake some shekels loose. How about it, Saul?"

"From what I've seen lately, our corporate community has come down with a severe case of compassion fatigue. I'll bet we can get some of them to help form a committee though. That's what something like this really takes."

"Great," said Claudia. "You handle the corporate angle and I'll take the grass roots. We'll need as many volunteers as we can get." Turning to her assistant Claudia continued, "Francis, as soon as this meeting's over, get the *Daily Record*'s editor on the phone. He owes me one and I bet I can get this story on tomorrow's front page."

The meeting was about to adjourn when Claudia looked over at her desk and spotted a package from Bob Beaumont. Its distinctive Paris Lites Cosmetics wrapping was easy to recognize. A few weeks ago, she had volunteered to be a "guinea pig" for Bob's new wrinkle cream. It couldn't have arrived at a better time, thought Claudia, as she turned back to the group. "By the way, as some or all of you may know, my fiftieth birthday is coming up, and I want NO ONE TO DO ANYTHING.

August 27th is going to be just a regular business day around here. If you feel you must, a card will be acceptable, but NOTHING MORE THAN THAT." Looking directly at Francis she added, "And I mean it, Francis."

"What did *I* say?" asked a slightly wounded Francis. "Did you see any birthday wrapping in my trash can? No, of course not. Why, there's not so much as one little cake candle hidden in my desk."

"Good. Let's maintain that level of consistency."

*   *   *

LOCAL COMPANIES JOIN TO SAVE SEALS

"Harry! Harry! I found it," shouted Josh, waving the Tuesday morning paper in front of his roommate's face and stabbing a finger at the headline. Putting the pillow over his head, Harry reached out and pushed the paper away. "Hey, I mean it. I found my new job. I'm gonna volunteer for these guys, meet lots of important people, show them what a hard worker I am, and somebody will hire me. Remember? I told you that's what the Captain and I came up with."

Harry lifted the pillow. "Go get 'em, tiger," he mumbled before sinking beneath the blanket.

Josh ran back out to the living room and grabbed the phone. He dialed the phone number mentioned in the article and was transferred to Claudia's assistant. Josh couldn't believe his luck when Francis told him that the company heading up the effort was a travel agency located in Cannery Village. The two hit it off immediately, and Josh promised to buy donuts for the committee's first meeting on Saturday morning.

*   *   *

By the end of the week, Francis had combined the list of grass roots volunteers with the one the corporate sales department had put together. This is a great start, Francis thought as he reached to answer his phone.

"Tell her this is Marine Bank calling and she's overdrawn," said the cheerful voice through the receiver. It was Ian West, the president of Marine Bank and Claudia's boyfriend.

"Hey, Ian, I'm really glad you called," said Francis. "With all this S.O.S. stuff going on, I haven't had a chance to get ahold of you."

"That's what happens when you work for a walking cause," said Ian, referring to Claudia's green streak.

"No kidding! But the reason I wanted to talk to you was that Claudia has put a death ray on *anything* for her birthday. I mean it. I think we'd better forget our idea of springing a surprise birthday party."

"Well, then, we'll just have to be really creative."

"Hello? Hello?" repeated Francis. "Ian, didn't you hear what I just said?"

"Sure, but you only turn fifty once. Don't worry. I'll take all the blame. Although . . . I'm still shorthanded here, so any help you can give me would really be appreciated."

"No problem, Ian," said Francis. "I'll see you at Saturday's S.O.S. kick-off meeting and we can talk more then."

*   *   *

Josh stood at the door of the main conference room and looked around in amazement. He had been handing out "HELLO! My Name Is" badges and trying to memorize the names and titles of the businesspeople who were sprinkled among a handful of local residents. To the left was the CEO of Tochelle Travel, Inc., the morning's host, speaking with the editor of the *Daily Record* and the senior vice president of marketing for TransWorld Insurance. The president of Marine Bank walked in with the assistant to the chairman of Software Ventures, Inc., while the director of personnel for Coast Manufacturing, Ltd., along with the chief financial officer of Bernard Construction Company and the head of Marine Environment Consultants had just sat down at the table. And right smack in the middle of everything were Josh's boxes of designer donuts, looking better than any professionally printed résumés.

Claudia opened the meeting by asking everyone to formally introduce themselves and give a brief description of their background or their interest in helping save the seals. When it was his turn, Josh explained that he was looking for a job and was happy to put in as much time as needed to help the effort any way he could. He gave a rundown of his education and past work experience, including copier shop clerk, construction, flower delivery, and catering experience—all of which brought a round of applause from the group.

"I think this means you've automatically been elected as the committee coordinator, Josh," said Claudia. "If you'd like, I'm sure Francis can find a desk and phone for you to use in our offices."

"That would be great."

When all of the introductions were concluded, the group set about finding a solution for the harbor's sea lions. According to the marine biologist, given the influx of seals and the growing harsh sentiments of those people who frequented the harbor's waters, the only really humane way to deal with the problem was to catch the seals and transport them to another area—all of which would take time and a good deal of money. It was decided that a public education campaign and a fund-raiser would be needed to accomplish the task ahead of them.

While the *Daily Record*'s editor could readily accommodate the need for public education with weekly columns written by the marine biologist, holding a fund-raiser was another matter entirely. Ian, along with the chief financial officer of Bernard Construction Company, offered to underwrite the benefit. Everyone agreed that given the time required to prepare the benefit, assemble guest lists, and mail invitations, the party's actual date would have to be somewhere around the end of August.

"How about August 28th?" asked Ian. "It's a Saturday."

Eyeing her boyfriend with just a hint of suspicion, Claudia answered, "Okay. But what type of fund-raiser should we be looking at?"

"Wait a minute," said Josh. "I completely forgot, but just as I was walking through the courtyard, I ran into a friend of mine who gave me a note. He said it'd come in handy for our meeting."

"Josh, I thought you said that you didn't know anybody in town," said Francis.

"Oh, this is a great guy I met here last Friday. Maybe you know him. Everybody calls him Captain."

"*Know* him? Anyone who works here knows the Captain," said Francis. "But," he said thoughtfully, "no one knows very much. What do you know about him, Josh?"

"Oh, Francis," Ian interrupted. "Don't you know the Captain owned the factory that was here before this place became Cannery Village? When he sold it to the developers he kept the land. His rental income must be incredible."

"I don't think that's so," said the CFO of Bernard Construction. "First of all, I think it was a fish cannery, not a factory. I used to know the acquisition manager who worked for the original developers. Seems to me they had to negotiate with an estate that held the property. As I recall, the estate was pretty tricky to deal with too."

"Bob Beaumont once told me that he thought he was a retired captain of industry—the former head honcho for some international brokerage firm or something. Guess he made a pile of money and decided he'd like to help other people do the same," said Claudia.

"Maybe that's where he got the seed money for Paris Lites Cosmetics," suggested Ian.

"Maybe," said Claudia with a shrug. "Maybe not. Maybe the Captain is just a group hallucination, the physical realization of a money angel that every entrepreneur prays for. Then again, maybe he's just a nice man who makes a lot of sense."

"What's the note say, Josh?" asked Ian.

Josh opened the slip of paper and read the note's two words aloud, " 'Visualize Fishing.' " With everyone watching him, Josh said, "I think he means find Word Bait by visualizing the problem. Sorta like boats use radar."

"And on that note," said Ian, "I suggest our new coordinator brush up on his visualization techniques so he can lead us at our next meeting." Turning to Francis, he added, "Can I see you for a few minutes before we break up?"

"Sure," answered Francis.

*   *   *

The following Monday morning, Josh walked up to his new desk at Tochelle Travel and found a handwritten letter on the Captain's familiar notepaper:

My Dear Josh,

Congratulations! Now that you have proven yourself an able fisher, it's time you teach others. Before you is the problem of creating a successful fund-raising event. You solve problems by coming up with new ideas, so angling for solutions, or ideas, is one and the same. However, this time, I suggest you employ the technique of visualization. Visualizing a set of events that are specific to a problem is an excellent way in which to solve it. Through visualization you will be able to remember— hook—a variety of additional Word Bait. Think of it as another technique to bring in even bigger and better Word Bait to help land your Catch.

Consider this problem: Sometime between 7 p.m. last evening and 7 a.m. this morning, you lost your set of keys to Harry's apartment. You have searched in every possible spot, but to no avail.

Many folks who find themselves in this position sit down in a comfortable chair, close their eyes, take a few deep breaths and try to *visualize, to "see," their steps from the last moment they remember having the keys. They keep the Word Bait of <u>keys</u> in mind as they review each step. Others, who may be more auditory than visual, will not be able to clearly "see" with their mind's "eye," but they will "hear" their mind's "voice" reminding them of every step they took since they last had their keys. Nonetheless, both types of individuals will remember a set of events that is specific to their problem—walking up to the front door, entering the living room, answering the phone. Did they have the keys with them then?*

Think of visualizing as turning on your own mental camcorder. You have already recorded the information, now you will simply be playing it back. As you said, it's "sorta like radar," only this time, you will be looking for Word Bait.

Good Luck, my friend!

Josh fired up his computer and wrote a memo about visualization based on the Captain's note. He sent a copy to each of the people who had volunteered for the Event Committee, asking them to spend a few moments before next week's meeting visualizing the best party they had ever attended, and to make a list of everything they could recall about it. Josh promised that this would get their initial effort off to a great start.

The day before the meeting, he had received a handful of lists. Josh added his own and sorted through them, picking out the minnow-sized Word Bait and preparing a Bait Bucket that read:

fireworks display	balloons	Cinco de Mayo
lion dance	cold beer	gourmet cuisine
scavenger hunt	door prize	boat parade
singing telegram	hors d'oeuvres	ticker-tape
flowers	ice carving	ballroom
parade rest	pinata	brass band
string popcorn	portable toilets	sing along
best costume awards	yacht club	celebrity roast
pop out of a cake	open bar	champagne
	anticipation	picnic
bob for apples	block off street	fashion show
string quartet	Ascot Races	lawn party
amusement park	clambake	blanket toss
	toga party	

It was decidedly an eclectic group.

*   *   *

At the appointed hour, the half-dozen members of the Event Committee assembled in Tochelle Travel's main conference room. Josh handed out the list, explaining how they were going to go fishing for some exciting concepts that would make the S.O.S. benefit one of the best parties ever.

As a warm-up practice, Josh had everyone join in gathering bigger Word Bait using their combined list as a starting point. Then they went after their Catch. Here's how:

> boat parade—nautical. "Hey, the benefit is for seals so let's make the **theme marine**."

> clambake—beach. "Why not hold the event **at the beach**? And make it the very beach where we'll try to catch the seals before transport?"

portable toilets—"Definitely."

ballroom—indoors. "We can put up a **big tent** with a **dance floor**."

brass band—"The **Marine Band**. What else?"

best costume awards—masquerade. "People could come as their favorite **fish** or **marine character**."

doorprize—giveaway. "Let's have **drawings** through the evening to give away **donated items**."

parade rest—parade. "We'll open the evening with a **grand procession** of all the guests in costume. And it will be led by the Marine Band!"

The committee was off and running. Josh next asked them all to take a moment and visualize the future event. "Just close your eyes, and imagine you're entering the party tent. What do you see? What do you hear or smell? What do the tablecloths feel like? How are the walls decorated? Is anything on the ceiling? How are the chairs and tables arranged? Where's the dance area? Is there a dais? And while you're looking around, just call out whatever you see. I'll take notes."

"**Huge aquariums** line the walls."

"We can get them donated for the **raffle**! Or, better yet, we'll hold an **auction**."

"All the tables are round, arranged in a big circle, and in the center are huge **ice carvings of seal lions atop a buffet table** that's sitting on a round stage."

"The buffet is full of **fresh seafood** like sashimi, shrimp cocktails, caviar, and salmon, set off with big **clam shells** and **boats of vegetables**."

"On both sides of the room are **Sand Bars** where guests can buy their drinks."

"Each table has a centerpiece of **flowers** springing from a **treasure chest**."

With everyone eagerly contributing, the meeting raced by.

*   *   *

In the following weeks, Josh taught all of the S.O.S. team how to fish for new ideas. Even though he'd taken a part-time job at TransWorld Insurance, reports of his success as a leader and hard worker filtered back to Claudia, who, given her own hectic schedule, had turned the entire project over to him.

The last few days before the benefit dinner were all but a sea of confusion at Tochelle Travel. Numerous waterscape paintings donated for the auction had been laid aside every available wall space. Marine artifacts and sculptures took up temporary residence in almost every office including Claudia's, which was stuffed with a captain's hailing trumpet, a ship's saloon chair, mounted shells, assorted scuba gear, and at last count, one surfboard.

"This is quite a haul, Josh," said Claudia, pointing to the various items strewn about her office. With only one more day to go before the benefit, she and Josh had gotten together for his last activity report. They ran through their checklists and Claudia noticed that Josh hadn't missed a thing, all the way down to the party favors: mini goldfish pinatas.

"Just one last item," noted Josh. "To give our Decoration Committee enough time to do their job, the tent is being put up this afternoon. How about dropping by after work to take a look at it?"

"I'd be happy to."

A little after six o'clock that evening, Claudia drove to the beach parking lot. As she started toward the immense white tent, the nearby fog horn let off with one, two, three, four, five blasts.

Claudia looked toward the tent and began to laugh. Just above the closed double-flap entrance was a sign that read "No Life Guard on Duty." She pulled aside one of the flaps and peered into the darkened interior. All she saw was a circle of light bright enough for a Fiji sunset. Then, suddenly the entire tent lit up and she saw Ian in a King Neptune outfit standing above a fully lit birthday cake and surrounded by five sea lions. Claudia saw seahorses dancing on the walls, a tremendous net of colorful balloons hanging from the ceiling, a huge white sand dune that was full of treasures for lucky raffle winners, and—her Aunt, dressed in an angel fish costume. Led by the Marine Band, the voices of hidden guests joined in raucous chorus and began to sing "Happy Birth—"

"Oh, God," said the birthday girl, "Oh, God!"

The combination gala benefit/surprise birthday party was a roaring success.

Word Bait Lesson No. 4

Visualize fishing? Absolutely. People spend a good deal of their day visualizing problems whether or not they realize it. Ever have a vivid dream? Bet you could almost recall each and every detail in the morning's light. Ever get caught day dreaming? That's visualizing with your eyes wide open. In a sense, visualizing is like dreaming; in both cases, you're watching a scene unfold. The difference is that when you're daydreaming, random thoughts fill your mind's eye. But when you try to solve a problem by visualizing it, you're *focused* in on "seeing" everything associated with that problem. That's why you can get an immediate boat load of Word Bait. It's another technique to help you fish for that Big Idea. And you can use it whenever you want!

To try it for yourself, sit in a comfortable chair, close your eyes and relax. Take a few deep breaths, concentrating on your breathing until nothing else clutters your mind. Then, imagine you're reliving this morning. Do you see getting breakfast ready? From left to right, what does the kitchen look like? Did you lock the front door on your way out? Did you drop your clothes off at the dry cleaners? What did the person who helped you look like?

Some people function on a visual level: They'll say, "I see what you mean." Others function on an auditory level: They'll say, "I hear what you mean." So even if you don't actually "see" these things in your mind's "eye," you'll "hear" your mind's "voice" respond with associated concepts.

During visualization, you can also employ your imagination. While you're sitting with your eyes closed, pretend you're all alone on a boat at sea. The boat has sprung a leak. What are you going to do? Why, look around, of course, to find out what your options are. Do you see a piece of cloth or any material that you can seal the leak off with? How about a radio, rubber raft, life jacket, or a bucket? Are the window curtains a bright color? Could you use them for signaling? Are the flares in the cabinet by the galley sink, or are they stowed under the bench seats? Do you see the cushions? Could they become flotation devices?

Again, for many people, rather than mentally "see" these things, they'll mentally "hear" them, such as: "There's a tablecloth. I could use that to try and stop the leak."

You see? Everything you've ever experienced through your five senses is recorded in your memory. You can either play back or imagine a scene through visualization. The solution to the next Exercise is already in your own mental camcorder. Take a look!

Hook, Line & Sinker

Students of all ages can fish:

The University of Southern Maine largely serves a student base of working professionals who want to "pick up another degree." As such, the usual esprit de corps that most universities enjoy was sorely lacking. "Students basically just showed up because they had to, not because they wanted to," notes university director Greg Bazinet. "We realized that in order for the university to grow, we first had to help students feel good about being here rather than somewhere else." With that in mind, Greg assembled a group of students and faculty members who looked at the problem through the eyes of the students. As a result, they decided that the perception of the classroom experience needed to be changed from one of "just learning a lesson" to one of "personal opportunity." Now, students are encouraged to bring their own company's problems into the classroom. Then, fishing along with fellow students, they are challenged to solve these problems and evaluate their solutions. Greg notes that, "We've been able to transform the classroom experience from being 'boring' into being 'stimulating.' Our students are actually excited about coming to class."

Word Bait Exercise No. 4

You're giving a sit-down dinner for 50 next Saturday. Don't worry, it'll be the perfect party, where everyone you had to invite but didn't really want to decided *not* to show up. Nevertheless, you have a formidable task ahead of you. What will you feed the faithful?

Time to turn your fish-finding radar on and take an imaginary stroll down your favorite grocery aisles. With paper and pencil in hand, spend the next 15 minutes in your mind's supermarket. What do you see when you walk in? The bakery department? What kinds of baked goods are there? Jot them down, then move on past the stacked rows of edibles.

By the way, just writing down chips and dips will not a dinner make; and for this exercise, please avoid the deli section. Once you've filled up your Bait Bucket by writing down everything you saw, take another 15 minutes to mix and match your Word Bait. Maybe you could use one of those big round loaves of bread as a bowl to hold that gourmet soup you found in aisle seven. Or, how about creating a fruit centerpiece surrounded with cheeses? You get the picture.

Hook, Line & Sinker

Fishing with your mental camcorder opens a world of possibilities:

When Julie Johnson, Advertising Manager of The Pinnacle Newspaper in Hollister, California, wanted to boost ad sales, she created a special advertising section for weddings. Julie visualized the concept of <u>weddings</u> to identify a number of businesses she might sell ad space to. Among the many ideas that surfaced were <u>gown</u>, <u>toasting</u>, and <u>travel</u>. These larger pieces of Word Bait helped land her Catch of the day: **seamstress**, **winery**, and **travel accessory manufacturer**, all of whom purchased advertising in her special section.

SEVEN

That's Service:
Strategic Planning

Her Wagnerian voice split the evening's silence with its demand. "Vas ist mit das elevator?! Du are . . ."

Federico Hidalgo instantly hit the answering machine's rewind button. If Monica Tietze-Gude's was the first message of the day, the rest could only get worse. And worse could wait until later.

It was well past six in the evening when Cannery Village's property manager first set foot in his own office after showing rental space all day. He'd flicked on the lights, saw that his in-basket was overflowing, his desk was full of last evening's paperwork, and his answering machine's light was blinking. After cutting Monica off mid-sentence, he stood beside his desk, took a handful of papers from his in-basket and wearily began to review them.

Bob Beaumont wanted to know if there was more office space available in the building. A note scribbled on the Great Outdoors Apparel Company letterhead simply read, "The john on the fourth floor doesn't work—Oscar." There was an envelope from Mariners Bank and one from Lynch, Cahn & Dodge. He set those aside; he was in no mood to deal with bankers or lawyers. The Anchorage Antique Shop wanted to know why their electric bill had gone up so much. Francis from

Tochelle Travel couldn't get one of Claudia's windows open. And Alfred from the shelving company wanted to meet with Federico regarding an early termination clause in his office lease. Nothing but problems, and they always seemed to arrive by the freighterful.

Looking at the box on the floor that he hadn't had time to open, Federico closed his eyes and wondered what life would be like when the tenants discovered he'd finally bought a fax machine.

Startled by a soft rustling sound, Federico opened his eyes. Standing before him was the Captain, a styrofoam cup in each hand. Three months earlier, when he was hired as Cannery Village's property manager, Federico had "inherited" the Captain. Even though his new friend worked directly for the developer/owners, Federico thought of him as a co-worker.

"I noticed your office lights on and thought perhaps you might like a cup of Sylvie's special blend."

Federico's fatigue finally gained the best of him. He sank into his chair. "The only thing I'd like better would be another fishing lesson on the Six Universal Questions."

"How so, my friend?"

Pointing to the remains of his in-basket, Federico said, "Well, you know, the Village's last property manager didn't pay too much attention to the bottom line. The vacancy rates for the commercial and office space were too high and customer services were terrible. I want to turn all that around, but the competition always seems to be one step ahead of me.

"So, just like you taught me, I took my initial pieces of Word Bait, customer service and competition, attached them to the

Six Universal Questions, and went fishing. What I came up with was the idea that if I got a fax machine tenants wouldn't have to drop notes on my desk. It took me a month to scrape together enough money just for that. And now I think it'll only be another way to *get* problems, not to *solve* them.''

''I see,'' said the Captain as he handed Federico one of the cups. ''Well, it would appear that you might not have fished quite deep enough. The Six Universal Questions are an excellent start. However, what you are attempting to solve is really a multifaceted problem. It takes into consideration every aspect of the business, including its future. Therefore, what you are in fact trying to do is create a strategic plan for the Village. So what you need, my friend, are Strategic Planning Questions.''

''But strategic planning includes everything! How can I possibly begin to do all that?''

''As your main concerns at the moment entail customer service, competition, and the profit that will flow from properly reviewing the first two, I suggest you start there.'' Setting down his cup, the Captain pulled a folded sheet of paper from his shirt pocket. ''I happen to have a list of Strategic Planning Questions for each of those specific items right here.''

Federico reached across the desk for the paper and opened it. He read the first question out loud. ''In what different ways do various customers use your service?''

''As you answer the questions,'' added the Captain, ''remember to keep your initial Word Bait of <u>customer</u> <u>service</u> and <u>competition</u> in mind.''

The property manager leaned back in his chair. ''Sometimes I lease new office space, sometimes I renegotiate leases, sometimes I have the plumbing repaired, sometimes I do little favors like tracking down a tent for the S.O.S. party, and sometimes, I give the store tenants tips on their advertising."

"The next question is?"

" 'What other forms of your product or service exist?' Well, that's one of my big headaches! There are high-rise office buildings downtown and a few stand-alone single or double-story complexes by the harbor. Some of them have a mix of commercial or restaurant space."

"You're fishing like an old salt now," said the Captain. "Go ahead, hook your initial concepts from the problem itself onto the Strategic Planning Questions and see what bigger pieces of Word Bait surface. You might also consider increasing your initial Word Bait to include profit, as that is your real goal. And, remember to—"

"Write down the answers?"

The Captain pushed his bifocals back into place. "Exactly, Federico. Exactly."

As the Captain left, Federico looked at the page of questions again. He quickly reached for Oscar's note, turned it over, and wrote down his initial Word Bait—customer service, competition, and profit. Keeping them in mind, he began to write down his answers to the Strategic Planning Questions.

1. For this kind of product/service, what is the competitive environment?

   Extreme. Most potential tenants are somewhat aware of the marketplace.

2. What are your competitors' strengths and weaknesses?

Downtown Locations/Strengths: More central location, closer to the <u>airport</u>, and <u>local</u> <u>services</u>.

Harbor Locations/Strengths: <u>Cheap</u> <u>rent</u>.

Downtown Locations/Weaknesses: <u>Congested</u> <u>area</u>, <u>glass</u> <u>buildings</u>, <u>no</u> <u>charm</u>.

Harbor Locations/Weaknesses: Scattered around and don't have the sense of <u>community</u> that the Village has.

3. What peripheral companies might you have overlooked as competitors?

<u>Independent</u> <u>leasing</u> <u>agents</u>.

4. How are your most successful competitors alike?

They <u>advertise</u> a lot.

Federico looked at the next question and shook his head. He knew the answer only too well.

5. What is the worst that your competition might do to you?

<u>Lower</u> their <u>rent</u>.

6. Could you form a strategic alliance with other companies to help decrease the impact of this?

Try a <u>promotional</u> <u>alliance</u> with the other <u>harbor</u> <u>office/commercial</u> <u>sites</u>.

7. From the customer's standpoint, what are the best improvements you could make in service and satisfaction?

Federico immediately thought of Monica, and wrote:

Handle their <u>problems</u> <u>first</u>. <u>Everyone</u> wants something a little <u>different</u>.

8. Which of your competitor's services could you copy or adapt to your own situation?

Office cleaning and security.

9. How could you get customers involved in using a service regularly?

Let them know how others use the service.

10. How well does your current customer service live up to its name?

Fat chance. They all complain at once. No way to keep up.

11. Do you have a "secret shopper" program to check on customer satisfaction?

The Captain looks after people.

Having filled up the back of Oscar's note, Federico reached for the Lynch, Cahn & Dodge envelope, flipped it over and wrote down just the new Word Bait he had brought in with the Strategic Planning Questions.

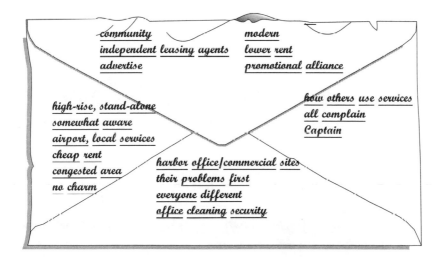

His Bait Bucket full, Federico sensed that a great idea might be lying dead ahead. Disregarding the late hour he took another sip of Sylvie's coffee, pulled a fresh writing tablet from his desk drawer and started after his Catch.

He jotted down high-rise, stand-alone and contemplated it for a moment or two. These pieces of Word Bait didn't seem to attract anything worth reeling in. But he kept at it, moving to his next piece, somewhat aware, fishing deeper and deeper until he hooked his first idea.

Thinking aloud, Federico said, "A **brochure**. Yeah, but just for now I could do a **low-cost flyer!**"

The second idea surfaced immediately. Then the third, and the fourth. Federico wrote down each of them as quickly as they came to mind.

> airport services: **Contract** with local **shuttle service** for tenants! We'd get small override payment. The shuttle could pick up dry cleaning and groceries, too.

"Hey! Why not work this backwards?" said Federico, as he began to write: Make the shuttle a service to **area residents** who want to visit the Village. We take an override here, too.

> cheap rent: No way! But, maybe give **potential tenants** (even **current tenants**?) **discount coupons** for items, even meals, sold in the Village. We'd get a percentage of the sale from the various shops. How about handing coupons out to **shoppers**, too?

> congested area/no charm: **Highlight openness** and **charm** in all printed materials.

community: The Village should become a **destination**, a **community center**. A place where people come to enjoy an afternoon. Good visibility.

independent leasing agents: **Split** the **rental commission** with outside agents and free up my time to attend to customer service and marketing.

advertising: Promotions. **Rent** the **courtyard** out in the evening for events? Great income, great visibility, and cheap advertising!

"Wow! This is incredible!" said Federico before he read the next piece of Word Bait and shuddered a bit. Lower rent. He bypassed this piece and moved on to the next one.

alliance: Form a **co-op ad campaign** with our shops and restaurants. They would all contribute, and we'd get a little money for managing it. We'd include notices of available office space in the ads! **Co-op promotions**, like sidewalk sales, maybe help support a local charity. (Free press!)

their problems first: Make tenants think their problem comes first. **First come**, **first served**. All handled in **24 hours**.

Federico looked over at the still unopened box on the floor and added: All **complaints/questions** to be **faxed** in. They won't have to walk into my office, and the fax will time-stamp complaints.

everyone different: People want customized service. Like the shuttle, we could **contract** with a **concierge** service. We'd get a little override on their earnings and I'd be free to do my work.

<u>office</u> <u>cleaning/security</u>: Again, we **subcontract** out **cleaning** and **security** and get a little override.

<u>how</u> <u>others</u> <u>use</u> <u>service</u>: Tell people about these new services. I could do a **monthly** desktop **newsletter** on my computer, with true success stories of how people use and like the new services.

<u>all</u> <u>complain</u>: Provide **preprinted complaint forms** to be faxed in.

<u>Captain</u>: He's always concerned about everyone. I should **speak** with **each tenant once a month** to see if they're happy.

Federico reviewed his Catch:

Low-cost newsletter, flyer for now

Contract with shuttle service for tenants, also area residents

Discount coupons for tenants, potential tenants, and shoppers

Highlight openness and charm

Make the village a destination, community center

Split rental commissions with independent leasing agents

Rent out the courtyard

Tenant co-op ad campaigns and promotion campaigns

Complaints are first come, first served, and all handled in 24 hours

Complaints/questions faxed in

> **Contract with a concierge service, office cleaning, security services**
>
> **Contract with office cleaning, security services**
>
> **Monthly computer desktop newsletter**
>
> **Preprinted complaint forms**
>
> **Speak with each tenant every month**

Federico realized that he'd hooked ways to improve customer service, catch up to the competition, and increase profits at the same time! Leaning back, he stretched out his arms, enjoying his moment of triumph like a long-distance runner who had crossed the finish line first. He grabbed the empty styrofoam cup, tossed it into the trash, and left for home—all the while making mental action plans for his Big Ideas.

Word Bait Lesson No. 5

Naming a new product, developing a new service, solving an interpersonal problem, finding a new job, and creating a birthday party—you've seen how angling for new ideas can quickly create viable solutions for a variety of tasks. But can it help with something as complex as strategic planning?

A Strategic Plan, like a company, is a system composed of inter-related subsystems. In addition to the customers and competition, the subsystems also include management, communication, finance, legal, product and service, marketing and promotion, facilities and production, contingencies, and sales. By addressing these subsystems individually, you can create a separate plan for each that will then be interconnected with those of the others. A change in any subsystem will affect the entire system, making your plan a unique and living entity in and of itself. This dynamic aspect of Strategic Planning requires periodic fishing among the subsystems to help keep the company on course.

Most people who haven't been involved in strategic planning are initially intimidated as it requires them to have a vision of where they want their organization to be in, say, three to five years. However, strategic planning is no more difficult than fishing for any new concept. Just remember to take one subsystem at a time. Piece by piece, the puzzle will fit together.

Hook, Line & Sinker

Fishing can turn a goal into reality:

The Renaissance of Discovery™, a summer <u>camp</u> where a child's imagination is immersed in a sea of <u>multimedia</u> <u>enchantment</u>, once was just an idea in the back of Robert Wood's mind. In order to develop this concept further, he cast his Word Bait into Strategic Planning Questions. "I immediately started to pull in new concepts for services, marketing, facilities, and personnel—almost faster than I could write them down. No one ever told me Strategic Planning could be fun!" Robert's summer camp opened in June 1995.

Word Bait Exercise No. 5

As a business is nothing without customers, their subsystem is the foundation of all strategic planning. Therefore, the needs and wants of the purchasing public should be your foremost concern. In the long run, the organization that thrives is the one that best satisfies those who buy its products or services.

Listed below are a number of Strategic Planning Questions to specifically help you better understand your customers. Whether you're the Chief Executive Officer or the Head Mail Room Clerk, attach the Word Bait from the problem "How do we improve sales?" to the following Strategic Planning Questions. After all, people who can solve problems are the most likely to ensure their company's success as well as their own. And who knows? Maybe you'll boost that bottom line or get that promotion sooner than you thought.

By the way, strategic planning isn't something that's just restricted to business endeavors. You should consider developing a personal strategic plan for your own future too! As it does in the corporate environment, a strategic plan will give you a road map for attaining goals. Now is as good a time as any to develop it. Keep in mind the pieces of Word Bait that define your goals while answering the questions below as if *you* were the product or service and the customers were people who can help you achieve them.

Spend the next 20 minutes answering the following questions in relation to your organization's product or service, writing down the bigger Word Bait that surfaces in the process. Then take another 20 minutes and go fishing for some really Big Ideas. To develop your personal strategic plan, follow the same process!

1. What qualifies a person as a prospective customer for this product/service?

    What purchasing power?

    What decision-making power?

    What degree of interest?

    How quickly should the person be able to reach a decision?

2. Who most often makes the decision to buy this type of product/service? Is it the person who will be using it?

   Who else influences the purchasing process (such as a gatekeeper)?

   Who is the end user?

3. What problem is the customer trying to solve, for which the product/service is a solution?

   As you analyze the customer's problem, what clues do you gather about the product benefits you should stress? What clues about your product/service features are there to point out?

4. Over the past couple of years, what changes have you noticed in your customers: For example:

   What changes in discretionary income?

   What changes in knowledge, education, sophistication, awareness?

   What new interests?

   What new worries?

   What new expectations about products/services? For instance:

   How has their definition of "quality" changed?

   What former luxury is now considered a necessity? Or what former "extra" do customers now expect as a matter of course? Does this give you a clue to their future expectations?

5. How might your customers continue to change, and why?

   How do you expect them to change, and why?

   What provisions should you make in preparation for the changes?

6. Which type of customer should be your first priority in planning, and why?

   Should your emphasis be on attracting the customer, keeping the customer, or both?

7. Which type of customer should be your second priority in planning, and why?

   Where should you place your emphasis?

8. Which type of customer should be your third priority in planning, and why?

   Where should you place your emphasis?

9. Whom do you expect your choicest customer to be two years from now?

   Whom do you expect your choicest customer to be five years from now? Ten years from now, and beyond?

10. What is the "lifetime value" of a customer?

11. How would you describe the relationship you've developed with your customers?

    What can you do to strengthen this relationship?

12. How loyal are your customers? How many think of you as their supplier and would rather do business with you than with anyone else?

    How many repeat customers do you have, and why do they return?

    What purchase or behavior pattern have you noticed among your repeat customers?

13. What can you do to encourage greater loyalty? Consider:

differentiating your product/service or company more clearly from the competition

doing a better job of targeting a niche market

making customer satisfaction a priority; following through with better service

listening to your customers more carefully; showing them greater interest and appreciation

14. How many new customers have you gained during the past year?

    Why have they decided to do business with you?

15. How many customers have you lost, and what have been their real reasons for dropping you? How do you know?

    How can the loss of customers be prevented?

16. What general dissatisfaction have customers expressed, and what is your source of information?

17. Do you have a recent study of customer satisfaction? Why or why not?

    If you've not formally inquired about customer satisfaction: what would you want to find out?

    Would the information be worth the expense?

18. What have your customers been asking for recently?

    Which customer requests seem to hold the greatest potential, and why?

19. Do prospective customers already understand this product, or do you also have to sell them on the idea behind it?

If marketing is an educational process: how do you know that your prospects are ready and willing to be educated?

20. Integrating what you know of the customer's needs and traits, what product/service benefits and features would you say are most meaningful to your customer? Such as, comfort, convenience, safety, design, efficiency, newness, power, speed, quality, size, status, service after purchase

21. What does the customer's philosophy of life or value system suggest about things to avoid mentioning?

    What images or features might turn the customer off?

22. Considering all you know about the customer's psychology, how appropriate is the tone of your message?

Hook, Line & Sinker

Fishing is a family affair:

"Hooking our Word Bait to Strategic Planning Questions shortened a corporate retreat from three days to one. Angling for concepts this way makes it so much easier to resolve specific issues," says health care consultant Dr. Richard Davis. "Before the day was through, we'd developed key concepts, themes, and action plans."

Dr. Davis's daughter, Allison, is also an able fisher. A high school freshman, she uses this system to develop concepts that set the framework for her oral and written presentations. "It helps me get started faster," Allison said.

E I G H T

Smithfield Solution:
OCEANS, SEAS, and
TIDE POOLS

> *"Any man can make mistakes,*
> *but only an idiot persists in his error."*
>
> —Cicero

Yolanda Baccus didn't have prepackaged days: nice, neat little affairs she could open at eight in the morning and wrap back up at five in the afternoon, without so much as one non sequitur in between. To the contrary, ever since she had been named purchasing director for Fairweather & Company, a national consulting firm, her days had become a Gordian knot of non sequiturs.

One of her chief responsibilities was overseeing the construction of the company's new building in Smithfield, and it had turned into "one of those" projects. The problems had begun with the infamous groundbreaking ceremony that nearly became her ceremonial burial when the caterers didn't show up on time. And now the endless squabbles between the architect and the general contractor were driving her crazy.

The masts of two sail boats silently passed outside her fourth-floor window while Yolanda thought back over the morning's progress meeting with the building's architect, Tim Wallace. Nearly before the hellos were completed, he brought up the problem of Change Orders not being followed. "I faxed

Nick a Change Order to widen the side door along with field sketches and specifications for a new door. Do you know what he did instead? He widened the front windows!''

Nick Stombolis, the building's general contractor, and Tim Wallace Senior had worked closely together for many years. Since his father had retired, Tim Wallace Junior had taken over the company and apparently run into trouble with his people management style.

"Did the windows need widening?'' asked Yolanda.

"It certainly wasn't called for in the drawings or in the Specification Booklet.''

"Did you ask Nick about the Change Order you faxed him?''

"He said he didn't get it. But I don't believe him. Nick's making plenty of money from this job to keep him in fax paper. He's just out there doing whatever he pleases, like some sort of possessed carpenter. It's a wonder the walls are plumb. Speaking of which, I have my serious doubts about the plumber he selected, too. The pumps he installed for the entry statement, the wall of water cascading down one side of the front of the building, look far too small to do the job. And that gigantic air-conditioning unit he wants to put on the roof: 'You'll never see it,' he says. For crying out loud, Yolanda, that thing is nine feet tall! You won't be able to miss it. You'll see it from the side of the building. You'll see it from the back of the building. And you'll certainly see it from the front of the building!''

Attempting to keep the meeting in some sort of sequence, Yolanda asked, "What did Nick say about widening the side door?''

"You mean after he told me he never got the faxed Change Order?"

"Roughly in that time frame, yes."

"Oh, something about the mechanical engineer wanting something. I don't know," said Tim in disgust. "I don't trust two consecutive words out of that guy's mouth anymore."

Oddly enough, Yolanda found herself having the very same problem with Nick—and Tim. In a separate meeting, just the day before, Nick had told Yolanda his side of the story: "You know, Yolanda, that son in Wallace & Son A.I.A. isn't half the architect his father is. We just had a great air-conditioning unit delivered to the site. It'll do the job you need and cost less than the one Tim Junior wanted. What more could you ask? But, I guess *Mr.* Junior doesn't feel it's necessary to save his client money. Well, I do."

Tim and Nick's working relationship had ripped apart like a water balloon on impact. It was up to Yolanda to put the pieces back together and get the building completed on time.

As she reached for the phone, Yolanda heard the rooftop scaffolding winches start up. "The Captain's here," she thought. "That's perfect!" She turned toward the window just in time to see a safety line drop down. Leaning over the window sill, Yolanda looked up toward the electric scaffold and saw her friend securing the safety line's other end to his harness.

"Captain, you're just in time," she called out.

He nodded in agreement and called back, "Well, that is certainly preferable to being late!"

"I need to do some serious fishing for a solution. Could you spare a minute or two?"

"I always have time for you, Yolanda. I shall be right down," responded the Captain as he secured his harness and prepared to lower the scaffold to her window.

Within moments, the winches came to a halt. Agile as a man half his age, the Captain easily glided into Yolanda's office and settled into one of the guest chairs. After telling her secretary to hold all calls, Yolanda proceeded to explain the problem with Tim and Nick.

"So you see," she concluded. "They're basically both pointing fingers at one another and shouting 'Liar, Liar, pants on fire.' Naturally, I'm paraphrasing here."

Tucking his chin down a bit and raising a brow, the Captain smiled at Yolanda's grasp of the situation. "Am I correct in assuming that you have yet to directly confront either of these gentlemen?"

"Oh, absolutely. A direct confrontation lets the other fellow know he got my goat. And as a general rule, I never let anyone know where I keep it tied up!"

"Well, then," said the Captain. "Personality conflicts are as complex as the individuals themselves. And as with many problems, we need to pare it down into a more manageable piece. Perhaps we should start with what you feel is really necessary to solve this problem."

Yolanda studied her desk for a moment. "Information. I don't even have enough of that to ask the right questions."

"Excellent!" The Captain leaned forward. "Yolanda," he said. "How would you like to learn an entirely new fishing technique?"

"You bet!"

"Then, I suggest that we try casting our lines in the hierarchical categories of OCEANS, SEAS, and TIDE POOLS, where we'll find *a virtually endless selection* of places to fish for a solution."

Yolanda knew all about fishing for solutions with Word Bait. The Captain had been her able teacher on several occasions. But OCEANS, SEAS, and TIDE POOLS? These were new angles.

The Captain began by reminding Yolanda how the human mind stores information—words—into clusters of categories—topical categories, and that what category a word is in is based on how closely it's associated with other words in the category. He explained that the more categories of associated Word Bait a person could identify, the quicker a solution, or a new idea, could be found. "For instance, the word Dog would be stored in the topical category of Family Pets. Dog most certainly would not be stored in the category of Metals and Alloys. I realize you are aware of this, Yolanda; so please, if you will, simply bear with me for a moment."

She nodded.

"These topical categories are arranged in hierarchies. At the top are the major categories, the OCEANS, which are the most general, then SEAS, and then the lowest and most specific level—the eight TIDE POOLS."

The Captain took out his notepad and wrote the hierarchy of associations like this:

OCEANS
Animal

SEAS
Family Pets—Dog

TIDE POOLS
Varieties/Examples
People/Animals
Things/Places
Parts
Abstractions/Intangibles
Verbs
Activities/Events/Processes
Descriptors

Yolanda reviewed what the Captain had written. "I understand why you wrote TIDE POOLS in the plural form, but why did you do the same for OCEANS and SEAS, where you have only one entry for each?"

"As you practice this type of fishing, you will discover that any piece of Word Bait may swim about in a number of SEAS and OCEANS. Dog, as an example, could be found in the SEA of Racing within the OCEAN of Sports. And in some cultures," continued the Captain, "Dog would even be found in the SEA of Cooking, under the OCEAN of Food."

"I get the point," said Yolanda with a grimace.

Returning to his notepad, the Captain wrote down a piece of Word Bait for each of the TIDE POOLS:

Varieties/Examples
circus dog

People/Animals
dog catcher

Things/Places
carpet

Parts
puppy teeth

Abstractions/Intangibles
animal magnetism

Verb
chew

Activities/Events/Processes
dog bath

Descriptors
affectionate

"I'm certainly glad you didn't write dinner next to Activities/Events/Processes," noted Yolanda.

The Captain looked at her and chuckled. "As with any endeavor, while angling for new ideas, you may occasionally feel stuck, stymied in trying to solve a problem. An excellent way to get started again is by broadening your Word Bait, looking at it from every level of the hierarchy. By doing so, you instantly multiply your opportunities for finding a solution. Shall we give it a go ourselves?'' he asked.

"I'm ready," responded Yolanda.

The Captain turned a page and wrote down a new hierarchy of OCEANS, SEAS, and TIDE POOLS. "What do you call the color of the blouse you're wearing?''

Yolanda looked at her sleeve. "Magenta, I think.''

He entered <u>magenta</u> in the Varieties/Examples TIDE POOL.

OCEANS

_____

SEAS

_____

TIDE POOLS
Varieties/Examples
<u>magenta</u>

"And, what would you say <u>magenta</u> is a variety or example of?'' asked the Captain.

"Well, it's an example of Red.''

"Exactly," said the Captain, writing Red in the space under SEAS and pointing to the hierarchy. "You have taken the Word Bait of <u>magenta</u> that was found in the TIDE POOL of Varieties/Examples and enlarged it to the category of Red. Now, expand the concept of Red.''

Yolanda thought a moment and smiled as she recognized the obvious answer. "Colors."

"You most certainly will find an Ocean of Word Bait related to magenta within the category of Colors!" The Captain wrote the new Word Bait in the space under OCEANS, completing the hierarchy like this:

OCEANS
Colors

SEAS
Red

TIDE POOLS
Varieties/Examples
magenta

"With magenta, we started at the bottom of the hierarchy and worked our way up. However, you could have easily started at the top and worked down. The human mind is as readily able to accomplish this 'looping' from bottom to top as it is from top to bottom. Let's see what happens with a very large concept such as People."

OCEANS
People

SEAS

_____

TIDE POOLS
Varieties/Examples

"How might you narrow People down into a smaller, more manageable category?"

Easy, thought Yolanda. "Men."

The Captain nodded, and wrote Men under SEAS. "And what would you put under the TIDE POOLS as a variety or example?"

Recalling the immature actions she had recently witnessed, Yolanda answered, "Caveman." Then, noticing the Captain's amused expression, she added, "Present company excluded, of course."

"A most gracious amendment."

OCEANS
People

SEAS
Men

TIDE POOLS
Varieties/Examples
Caveman

Leaning forward in her chair, she spread the Captain's notepapers across the desk. Yolanda was amazed. She knew the value of finding Word Bait in order to bring a solution to the surface, but the Captain had just given her an outline with which to delve into *every aspect* of her Word Bait. Using the hierarchies, she could fish deeper for a solution than ever before! "Let's try this on the Smithfield problem," said Yolanda.

"Delightful," concurred the Captain as he moved his chair closer. "For the purpose of this exercise, we will include the OCEANS. Although, in general, you will find them far too broad to deal with effectively. You'll see what I mean in a moment."

Keeping her problem with Tim and Nick in mind, they set sail for the Word Bait in associated OCEANS, SEAS, and TIDE POOLS. Yolanda took a yellow writing tablet from her desk and wrote OCEANS at the top. Since Information seemed to be an overriding concern, they picked that as their OCEAN, and Yolanda entered it in the hierarchy.

"As it is, that OCEAN includes anything from speeches and libraries to telecommunications. So you see it needs to be tamed into more manageable pieces. Which aspect should we concentrate on?"

"Background information," said Yolanda as she entered it underneath SEAS.

"Now let's look in some of the TIDE POOLS," said the Captain. "What Word Bait do you find in the People/Animals category?"

"Gossip!" said Yolanda. "Let me think; there would also be news reporter, informer, and, and messenger. Oh! I know a good one: reliable source."

After Yolanda entered these under People/Animals, the Captain asked her to fill in some of the other TIDE POOLS. Under Descriptors she wrote: inaccurate, slanted, detailed, confidential, and factual. Books and archives were placed below

Things/Places, and <u>lecture</u> and <u>Gallup</u> <u>Poll</u> were written beneath Activities/Events/Processes.

Yolanda fell silent as she reviewed her Word Bait hierarchy.

OCEANS
Information

SEAS
Background Information

TIDE POOLS
People/Animals
<u>gossip</u>
<u>news</u> <u>reporter</u>
<u>informer</u>
<u>messenger</u>
<u>reliable</u> <u>source</u>

Descriptors
<u>inaccurate</u>
<u>slanted</u>
<u>detailed</u>
<u>confidential</u>
<u>factual</u>

Things/Places
<u>books</u>
<u>archives</u>

Activities/Events/Processes
lecture
Gallup Poll

"Do you recall the two Word Bait Questions?" the Captain asked.

"Absolutely: What does this word make me think of? and How can I use it to solve my problem?"

"Excellent," said the Captain. "Next, cast for your Catch by applying those questions to each piece of bait you found in the TIDE POOLS."

"News reporter," said Yolanda, mulling the concept over in her mind. Then, with a laugh she added, "I need the facts all right, only in this case, it's the fax. I ought to get a copy of that Change Order Tim said he faxed Nick." Quietly fishing so as not to frighten her Catch away, Yolanda continued to concentrate. Her eyes moved swiftly from reliable source to detailed and then back again. "Aah," she whispered, "Christian Stone is the project's mechanical engineer. He certainly knows the details, and he'd be a reliable source if I could get him to talk." Fixing her gaze under the TIDE POOL of Things, Yolanda considered archives. Archives are full of things in the past, she thought. They're full of history! She made a mental note to call her predecessor, Herman Aune. He'd worked with Tim's and Nick's companies for years before retiring. Lastly, she cast her line into lecture. Then Yolanda lifted her eyes to meet the Captain's.

"Captain," she said in her best parental voice, "when I have this figured out, I will give them all a lecture!"

The Captain clapped his hands together. "And a splendid one it will be!"

The teacher and his student rose to congratulate each other. Before heading back to his scaffold, the Captain added, "Yolanda, my dear, should you be in need of my assistance again—"

"I know," she said waving good-bye, "you're always here when I need you!"

Yolanda returned to her desk, her Rolodex, and her phone. She picked up the receiver, punched nine, and spun the Rolodex to "S" while waiting for an outside line. Then she pushed seven buttons and sat back as the phone rang.

"Christian Stone here."

"Christian, it's Yolanda."

"Hi! What's going on?"

Yolanda was well aware that getting a person to discuss something they would rather not was a delicate, intimate ballet through the rhythms of half truth and distraction. In order to achieve a standing ovation, both partners could neither lead nor follow at the same time. Above all, both partners must avoid stepping on the other's toes. Nevertheless, she threw caution to the wind and stepped in with both feet. "That's what I was going to ask you."

She told Christian about the problems between Tim Junior and Nick, the missing fax, and her concern about completing the project on time. With Christian's response, the conversation took to center stage. He executed a stunning verbal entrechat, crossing his words back and forth in a blur of sense and nonsense before they landed in a perfect plié. Yolanda sidestepped his plié with a delicate arabesque, jeté, arabesque combination. While she stood on point, Christian began a quick step around the topic. This brought Yolanda to the conclusion that either she had to get him to join in a Grand Promenade or ask him if his slippers were too tight.

"Christian," she said, in her sweetest you-just-stepped-on-my-toes voice. "You're on-site almost every day, I'm not. There must be something you've seen or noticed that could help solve this problem." She heard an audible sigh. Yolanda and Christian were about to join each other in the Grand Promenade.

"A couple times a week I see Tim's dad and Herman Aune on-site."

"What was Herman doing there?" she thought.

"But I'm sure that doesn't mean anything," Christian said reassuringly.

Yolanda forced herself to remain casual. "Do you ever speak to them or see them speaking with anyone else?"

"Yeah, sure, we've even gone to lunch a couple of times."

Risking the possibility of tripping herself up, Yolanda asked, "So, what do you fellows chat about, just the building I guess?"

"Yeah, they're really interested. You know, it was the last project the three of them worked on together before Tim Senior retired from his architectural practice and Herman retired from Fairweather. But, hey, I'm sure it doesn't mean anything, Yolanda. Tim and Herman just don't know what to do with themselves. You know."

About to make her final curtsy before exit, Yolanda replied, "You're right. I mean . . . what are you going to do if you don't play golf?"

"Yeah, that's it!" said Christian, greatly relieved that she was seeing things his way.

Yolanda hung up the phone. A look of satisfaction crossed her face as she reached for the Rolodex again and searched through the A's, the S's, and finally the W's. With the Captain's help she had baited her hook and pulled in just the right Word Bait. Now she was about to drop a net around the solution.

Yolanda completed her calls to Herman Aune, Nick Stombolis, and Tim Wallace Senior, satisfied that each had agreed to meet with her late that afternoon. She told them that she wanted to personally discuss some problems regarding the Smithfield building. That much was the truth. However, she failed to tell them that anyone else had been invited to the meeting.

*   *   *

At 4:35 that afternoon, Nick Stombolis entered Fairweather & Company's lobby. At 4:37 Tim Wallace Senior entered the lobby. And at 4:50, Herman Aune walked through the front doors of a company he had come to love. In the midst of happily greeting one another, it came to light that each of them had a meeting with Yolanda Baccus—a 5:00 p.m. meeting.

"I hope she doesn't know we've been tinkering with Smithfield," said Herman.

"I hope she doesn't tell my son," said Tim Senior.

"I hope she doesn't fire me," said Nick.

At 4:59 Yolanda Baccus stood by her office window watching a magnificent cloudscape close her day in a Christmas-colored package of red and gold wrapping. Then she returned to her desk, called her secretary and said, "Bring the boys to my office."

Word Bait Lesson No. 6

You say you want a line-busting Catch? You say you want to be the envy of your colleagues, the target of your competitors, and the apple of your boss's eye? Then fish in every possible aspect of your Word Bait, whole new categories of it, that can tow you right to that great new concept or super solution. Fishing in the hierarchies is also an excellent way to get restarted anytime you're stuck.

As always, begin with your initial Word Bait from the problem. Write down a piece of it under the SEAS category. Don't be concerned with the OCEANS; while they are the top level of the hierarchy, they're often too broad to work with effectively. Fill in each of the TIDE POOLS. Then with the two Word Bait Questions in mind, go after bigger bait and your Catch! To see how, read through the following example from Lynch, Cahn & Dodge:

Whereas the law partners had determined, in essence and in fact, the validity of the prudence of originating new methodologies so as to enhance fiscal pro formas—which roughly translated meant, "We need to get more quid for our pro quo," it was decided that they would go on a fishing expedition to define new revenue-generating "opportunities" for their clients as well as for other law firms.

They began their effort by taking pieces of Word Bait from various aspects of their business, such as ceremonies, emotions, language, and computers, which then steered the way into SEAS that fed the TIDE POOLS full of great Word Bait. Listed here are the SEAS as they saw them. Underneath each, you'll note the partners selected a TIDE POOL. Under each of those is a piece or two of Word Bait that they used to haul their Catch on board.

1. SEA
Ceremonies

TIDE POOL
Activities/Events/Processes
funeral

CATCH: How about developing a type of cradle-to-grave **service** for our personal clients? For one flat, annual fee we would review all of their personal contracts like insurance policies and mortgages, as well as write wills and trusts and arrange for conservatorships.

2. SEA
Emotions

TIDE POOL
Verbs
comfort

CATCH: Sometimes clients could use **stress counseling**. How about this as a service?

3. SEA
Language

TIDE POOL

Verb

<u>translate</u>

CATCH: How about a pocket **Legal/English dictionary** that translates difficult-to-understand terms and concepts? This could be a marketing giveaway, a saleable reference book, and a product other law firms could imprint with their own name.

4. SEA

Computers

TIDE POOL

Varieties/Examples/Processes

<u>modems</u>

CATCH: For our corporate clients we could create a service that **downloads case law** that may affect their business directly, into their own computer.

5. SEA

Compete

TIDE POOL

Varieties/Examples

<u>trial</u>

CATCH: What about offering law firms a service in which we would be the **opposing counsel in mock trials**?

6. SEA

Controversy

TIDE POOL
Abstractions
<u>conflict</u>

CATCH: We could start a **monthly subscription newsletter** service for **updates** of legal issues regarding **specific industries**. We could sell this to clients and possibly to other legal firms for their own clients.

7. SEA
Easy

TIDE POOL
Abstracts/Intangible
<u>degree</u> <u>of</u> <u>difficulty</u>

CATCH: We could create and sell a **dos and don'ts pamphlet** on what to do and what to expect in **court**. This could also be a **video**.

8. SEA
Labor Relations

TIDE POOL
People/Animals
<u>administration</u>

CATCH: We could present **half-day seminars** on **labor relations administration**.

9. SEA
Forms

TIDE POOL
Abstractions
<u>conformity</u>

CATCH: Why not sell our corporate clients a **three-ring binder** of **form letters** and **agreements** pertaining to their industry? This could be **updated annually**.

10. SEA
Telecommunications

TIDE POOL
Varieties/Examples
<u>radio</u>

CATCH: How about doing a local call-in **radio show**? We could call it "Confer with Counsel" and maybe do a companion **column** in the local **newspaper**. These would be great marketing programs for our firm.

Congratulating each other on their angling ability, the partners shoved off for the accounting department to pirate some funds with which to launch their new "opportunities."

Hook, Line & Sinker

He fishes to music:

Every week, radio program directors in Texas, Oklahoma, Arkansas, Louisiana, Tennessee, Mississippi, and Florida receive CDs and promotional material from folks like Raymond McGlamery, a regional promotion director for Priority Records.

"I always have to do something special that will make our artists stand out. One of our groups had done a remake of 'I Only Have Eyes for You.' I fished around the TIDE POOLS and found Eye Chart, and that's what the promotion piece became! It read:

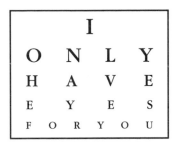

I			
O	N	L	Y
H	A	V	E
E	Y	E	S
F	O	R	Y	O	U

THE FUNKY POETS HAVE
THEIR EYES ON A HIT!

"I did the same thing for Clive Griffin's release of 'Commitment of the Heart.' By using the SEA of Commitment, I pulled up Contract in the Things/Places TIDE POOL. So I wrote a contract on parchment paper with burnt edges that read: I, _____, will agree to air Clive Griffin's record . . . That record got more air play in this market than any other. Now it's easy to be creative!"

Word Bait Exercise No. 6

You've just landed the prized "Puppy Loves" dog food account for your growing advertising agency. Now your challenge is to develop incredible concepts for a television commercial campaign that will justify your outrageous fees!

To give you a head start, all of the topical categories, SEAS, you could ever hope to sail across are listed in alphabetical order in Part 4: Fishing Tackle. Pick as many as you like that are associated with this problem. Fill in their TIDE POOLS with bigger Word Bait. Then go fishing! Here's how to set your lines:

1. With your problem in mind, creating concepts for <u>dog food</u> television <u>commercials</u>, select as many of the following SEA categories you like. For each ask yourself: What does this category make me think of? and How can I use this category to solve my problem? Should your line remain motionless for more than a moment or two, go on to the next SEA.

2. If you've hooked something, the first thought that bubbles up will be a piece of Word Bait from any of the eight TIDE POOLS: Varieties/Examples, People/Animals, Things/Places, Parts, Abstractions/Intangibles, Verbs, Activities/Events/ Processes, or Descriptors. Put your Word Bait in the appropriate category and fill in the rest of that TIDE POOL with more fresh bait. Continue this process for each of the TIDE POOLS. Then, select a piece of that new bait, and keeping it in mind, once again ask yourself the two word bait questions.

3. When you feel something on your line, bring up that great idea and write it down. Here are a few examples to get you started:

1. SEAS
Celebrate/Holidays/Parties/Parades

TIDE POOL
Activities/Events/Processes
<u>birthday</u> <u>party</u>

CATCH: Have a puppy opening a **wrapped present** that is full of **dog food**.

2. SEAS
Political Activism/Militancy/Social Change

TIDE POOL
People/Animals
<u>politician</u>

CATCH: Have a **dog** at a **podium promising** a bag of "Puppy Loves" in every kitchen.

3. SEAS
Decisions/Choices/Judgment

TIDE POOL
People/Animals
<u>judge</u>

CATCH: Have a **panel** of **dogs** in **judges' costumes, judging** the best dog food.

Now it's your turn. Give yourself 20 minutes to select one of the SEAS listed in Part 4 and fill in all its TIDE POOLS. Take another 20 minutes angling for your Big Idea.

N I N E

Speech! Speech!: Speech Writing

"Speech." Ian said the word "speech." Right there in the hallway he said it. It was preceded by "Write a" and followed by "I need it for the Chamber of Commerce meeting next week." The new Assistant to the President of Marine Bank didn't recall the rest of the details. His mind had become firmly stuck on that speech word. He walked into his office with Ians memo in hand and looked around for an idea . . . or an escape.

There were his diplomas on the wall, his favorite picture of Susie on the credenza, and his name plate on the desk clearly stating: JOSHUA FILIPACK. Being Ian West's assistant was a plum position. Josh was learning the banking industry from the inside out, meeting all the "right people," and loving the challenges.

In just his first few weeks he had wrapped up his S.O.S. commitments, arranged the local travel, accommodations, and entertainment for a contingent of overseas customers; helped resolve a nasty problem in the customer service department; and sat in on a Board of Directors and a Lending and Credit Policy Committee meeting. However, a speech—correction—writing a speech, was an entirely different kettle of fish.

Josh walked over to the windows facing the Village's courtyard. Across the way he saw a discreet "Under New Ownership" sign next to the gold and white awning above The Catch's front door. His thoughts wandered to the Captain. Josh had been so busy he only now realized that he hadn't seen the Captain since before the first S.O.S. meeting.

Maybe they're right, thought Josh. Maybe he is just a figment of everybody's imagination. On the other hand, his advice was sure real—and Josh was in need of real advice. He grabbed Ian's memo, put it in his leather folder, and headed for the espresso cafe.

As always, Sylvie was at her post greeting afternoon guests. "People are *still* talking about that party!" she said. "Just about everyone in the harbor knows your name now, Josh."

"Thanks. But there's only one name *I'm* interested in."

Sylvie pointed towards the reserved window table. "He's right where you left him."

Josh's face brightened. Clutching the folder, he went straight to the Captain's table whereupon his mood took a turn for the worse. Two freshly poured cups of Kona coffee had been placed on the table, but there was no sign of the Captain.

"I had assumed that a president's assistant would not have time for such momentary pleasures as coffee with an old friend," said the Captain.

Hearing the voice behind him, Joshua jumped. He turned around and saw the Captain, polka-dotted suspenders and all. Green and orange no less. "Am I glad you're here! You were such a great help with finding me a job, I wanted to know if . . .

if . . . Well, if you could help me write a speech too. I know they're completely different, but—"

"Quite the contrary, my friend. Finding a new job and writing a speech are more alike than not. After all, finding a new job is simply solving a problem and any type of writing is simply solving a problem on paper. I should say that the story about Jonah would be a bit of a tedious read if it weren't for his whale. And Red Riding Hood, if I may add, could not have reached legend proportions without her wolf problem."

"Afraid I'm not so lucky. I don't have a whale or a wolf, only a deadline . . . for this." Josh opened his folder and handed the Captain Ian's memo.

> TO: Josh
> FROM: Ian
>
> I need a speech, 10 to 15 minutes in length, to give at next week's Chamber of Commerce meeting. The meeting is an overview of the business community's environmental efforts. Let's shake them up a little and make it funny. When can I see the first draft?

"I must tell you, Josh," said the Captain, guiding his bifocals back into place. "I have reviewed much worse memos."

"I know," sighed Josh. "It's just that I'm a terrible writer. Even my high school English teacher told me I didn't know a metaphor from a two-by-four."

The Captain's eyes widened with delight. "Well, then," he motioned toward the deck chairs. "Shall we do a bit of fishing?"

"That's why I brought my Bait Bucket!" said Josh, opening his folder and pulling out a pen as they sat down.

"Do you recall that one of the steps we used to pull in ideas for finding you a job was to answer a few of the Six Universal Questions?"

"Sure."

"Well, then, we'll repeat that very process, with one exception. This time we'll use questions that are *specifically* designed to help solve the problem of writing a speech. All we need to do is attach the initial Word Bait from your problem, 'Write a humorous speech about the environment,' to some Speech Question lures. And you do that by remembering the initial Word Bait while you answer the questions. Shall we begin?"

"You bet!"

"Exactly what is the concern, or the issue of common interest, around which you might build this speech?" asked the Captain.

"The business community's need to continue supporting environmental efforts." Josh wrote down his answer.

"What different angle or slant on the subject will you use to attract and maintain the audience's attention?"

"Well, Ian wants it to be funny," said Josh, glancing toward the harbor. "So, it looks like I'm in need of a whale, or a wolf. Or, or . . . I got it! I could make it a mythical setting."

"What would be the most effective words to open the speech with—a stimulating question or perhaps an amusing story?"

Josh cast into <u>humorous</u> and <u>mythical</u>. "We're not in Kansas anymore," he quipped. "Wait a sec. You know, that's not bad." Then he dropped his line back into <u>environmental</u> and said, "The Land of Oz definitely predates acid rain. Hey, that's it! **What would the Land of Oz and the Emerald City look like if nobody cared about the environment?** *Captain*, you're a Wizard! It's a dynamite theme!"

"That it is! However, a theme is merely the start. Now we need a beginning, a middle, and an end," said the Captain, continuing with his questions. "Exactly what do you want your speech to accomplish? As a result of it, what do you wish the audience to understand?"

"That <u>people</u> can <u>make</u> a <u>difference</u>. People just like those that helped Save Our Seals. People just like those in the Chamber of Commerce meeting."

"What new point of view, or what different perspective, do you want the audience to gain? What attitude should they adopt toward the concept you present?"

Josh thought for a moment. "That we can't become <u>lazy</u>, expecting 'the other guy' to do something about preserving our environment."

"What conclusion do you want the audience to reach? What do you want them to do as a result of this speech?"

"I don't know, I guess I . . . Well, why not have them . . . I know! They should institute an <u>environmental</u> <u>awareness</u> <u>campaign</u> within their own companies."

"What could move this group to take such an action?"

"I think by making the speech fun, by making the job of protecting our environment fun; I think that would help in getting people involved."

"Such as the S.O.S. benefit?"

"Wait a minute," said Josh. "I think I've snagged something. The purpose of this speech should be to introduce an easy-to-follow environmental campaign for employees. Maybe an award program."

"What main points might you utilize to support this position?"

"I'll use Oz as a metaphor. In my Oz, everyone figured that 'the other guy' would do something about preserving the environment. As a result, the Land of Oz and the Emerald City became toxic waste dumps. Then, someone will show them how to work together, like a team, toward a single goal."

"Rather an 'e pluribus unum' effort?"

"Right. Part of that team effort will include this new award program."

"Mindful that the speech will present more than one main point: What type of sequence would be the clearest, the most persuasive, and the best to lead the audience into accepting your concepts?"

Setting his coffee cup down, the Captain added, "Should you select a sequence in chronological order, such as according to the passage of time; or step-by-step—a sequence in topical order, such as from the easiest to the most difficult; or, should it be a sequence in spatial order, such as according to places or according to parts of a whole?''

''I think I'll start in <u>Oz</u>. You know, set the stage, and then bring it into <u>reality</u>.''

''And, what transitional comment might connect these points?''

''I could use the <u>award</u> <u>program</u>, of course.''

''What do all of your points lead up to?''

''Instituting a <u>company</u>-<u>wide</u> <u>environmental</u> <u>award</u> <u>program</u>.''

''What will the audience gain by embracing this conclusion?''

''They'll get a <u>better</u> <u>place</u> to <u>live</u>, not to mention the <u>recognition</u> and <u>admiration</u> of their peers and employees,'' answered Josh as he reached for his coffee and awaited the Captain's next question.

''What might be the very last words of the speech? Would it be possible to tie those last words in with the first words of the speech?''

''If I <u>start</u> off in <u>Oz</u>, that's where I'll <u>wind</u> <u>up</u>.''

''What is the most memorable statement you might make that would refer to the heart of the message?''

''Maybe something along the lines that we don't have to accept the speech's mythical version of Oz. We can <u>control</u> our own <u>destiny</u>.''

"Perhaps you might conclude the speech with a call to action. What specific next step should your audience take, and by what date should they accomplish this task?"

"Well," said Josh, "we could have a sign-up sheet on hand for those people who want to get their companies involved in the award program."

"What tangible material might you leave behind for participants? Perhaps an outline on which they can make notes, a handout such as a summary or checklist, or some type of promotional material?"

"I don't know. I'll have to think about that."

"First," said the Captain, rising to leave, "I suggest you fill your Bait Bucket with enough related concepts to complete your speech. I believe you will find plenty of bigger Word Bait by fishing around Oz, awards, and toxic waste dump. Then you'll be well on your way to the open sea and your big Catch: a completed speech!"

"Thanks! The speech questions were great—I couldn't have done this without you."

As the Captain bowed his good-bye, Josh took a fresh piece of paper and created a column each for Oz, awards, and toxic waste dump. Ten minutes later, he'd hauled in the concepts that would fill his speech.

OZ	AWARDS	TOXIC WASTE DUMP
Toto	team	pesticides
Tin Man	committees	industrial waste
Dorothy Gale	banquet	landslides
Scarecrow	plaque	acid rain
Lion	Hall of Fame	smog
Wicked Witch	achievement	pollution
The Wizard	determination	DDT
ruby slipper	fame	oil slick
Emerald City	pride	ecology
Auntie Em and		ethics
Uncle Henry		

After reviewing his lists, Josh wrote the speech's opening sentence: **No doubt everyone in this room knows Dorothy Gale**. Then he wrote the second sentence: **Well, she called me a couple of months ago to see if I could give her some advice**.

The speech continued, relaying how everyone thought the First Wizard Deluxe would look after the environment. When he took off for the land of 'e pluribus unum' things took a turn for the worse. Acid rain so badly pitted the Emerald City in the County of Oz, it actually became orange. Pesticides killed the forests and flowers. The Tin Man's heart was so broken, he left for the coast. Then, on Ian's advice, Dorothy formed committees, putting everyone in charge of their own environment. She even created an award program.

Josh ended the speech with these words:

> **When all of this was done, Dorothy held a banquet for everyone who worked so hard. At the**

end of the evening she presented each guest with a ruby slipper, cut and polished from the finest glass, in recognition of their commitment.

You'll note that I have one of those very slippers in my hand right now. Taking a page from Dorothy's book, I suggest that we start our own mutual admiration society, encouraging everyone to help our common cause. Tonight I propose that we form a business grassroots society and encourage all of our employees to participate. You'll find details in the handouts at the front door.

If Dorothy were here, I'm sure she'd wrap up this speech by saying that working together we'll keep the sky blue right here in our own backyard!

Leaning back in the wood and leather deck chair, Josh grinned. He read the speech over. Then he read it again. And then, he took off for Ian's office.

Word Bait Lesson No. 7

The solution to any problem is just an idea. To find that idea, always start with initial Word Bait from the problem itself. Wrap that Word Bait around lures, but not just any lures—task-specific question lures—which in this instance are Speech Questions.

Imagine the different forms a speech could take depending upon your answer to this question: Will the audience be there to learn or mainly to socialize? If the audience is there to learn, the speech must educate. If the audience is there to socialize, then the speech must entertain. Will the audience be open-minded or skeptical? Are you going to be reinforcing friends or trying to convince the opposition? "Will hard facts, human interest stories, or role-playing be most convincing to the audience?" The answers to each of these questions will define and refine your speech, keeping it from going adrift.

Once you have the speech's structure, you'll want to fish a little deeper for the rich metaphors—like the ruby red slipper award—that will bring it to life.

Hook, Line & Sinker

Here's how one fellow won awards fishing:

A speech writer in Rochester, Illinois, John Hamm needed a vehicle that would allow him to weave a variety of concepts into one presentation regarding a social service agency's reforms. With his initial Word Bait John fished for concepts and came up with the metaphor of windows. Here's how he used it: John's Cashier's Window represented legislative and financial support; his Stained Glass Window introduced how different interests could fit together; a Bay Window stood for a broader view of the environment that also added value to the agency, as it does to a house; a Computer Window related to technology; and lastly, a Kitchen Window represented the social services that were directed into the homes of families.

John's speech won a Silver Quill Award and was a finalist in the Gold Quill Award category of the International Association of

Business Communicators. It also won a national award from the National Association of Government Communicators.

Word Bait Exercise No. 6

As a member of your local speech club, you've been assigned to give a talk on "Answering Machines and Me." What do you know about answering machines? Just about as much as your audience does!

Start with your initial Word Bait of <u>answering</u>, <u>machines</u>, and <u>me</u>. To establish the theme and structure, hook those concepts onto the following Speech Questions for the next 15 minutes, and see what lands in your boat.

1. Why will the audience be there?

   mainly to learn something they can use

   mainly to socialize, or to see and be seen

   mainly to be entertained

   mainly to be inspired or persuaded

   mainly to fulfill a duty

   it's a captive audience; they have no choice

2. If you'll be sharing the stage with other speakers, what do you expect their presentations to be?

   What topics will other speakers give?

   Any views that oppose or contradict your own?

What presentation styles will other speakers give—serious, humorous, dragging, fast-paced, super dynamic, direct, story-telling?

3. What do you expect their attitude will be toward the material you present?

curious, eager to learn

skeptical, critical

open-minded, receptive to different opinions

threatened, defensive if challenged

not interested

noncommittal, difficult to read

4. What forms of evidence will be most convincing to this audience? What kinds of specifics do they respond to?

examples; statistics; definitions; hard facts; details

direct comparisons and contrasts

indirect comparisons (analogies, metaphors)

testimonials and quotations

human-interest stories

results of experiments; case studies

models, prototypes; simulations; role play

actual hands-on experience

5. What different angle or slant on the subject (what premise; what point of view) will you use to get and keep the attention of this audience?

6. Exactly what do you want your speech to accomplish?

As a result of your speech, what do you want participants to understand?

What new point of view, or what different perspective, do you want participants to gain?

What attitude toward a subject do you want them to hold?

What skill do you want them to acquire?

What conclusion do you want them to reach?

What do you want them to do as a result of your presentation?

What could move this group to take such action?

7. What main points (not more than five) should you use to build your case?

    Main Point #1:
    Main Point #2:
    Main Point #3:
    Main Point #4:
    Main Point #5:

8. To open your presentation, what should be the very first words out of your mouth? (What would be the most fitting and effective attention-getting words pertaining to the heart of your message?)

    a call for audience participation or response

    a gimmick for shock value

    a reference to a historic event

    a relevant joke

    a relevant quotation

a specific compliment for the audience

a startling fact or statistic

a stimulating question

an amusing true story; a touching true story

an example or an illustration

9. Should your attention-getter be serious, amusing, or tragicomic?

   If you're the first speaker and there is no emcee: what sort of attention-getter will warm up the audience?

   How much time should you spend on the attention-getter as compared with the rest of the presentation?

10. To close your speech, what should be the very last words out of your mouth?

    What similar wording could tie the close to the attention-grabbing opener?

    If you opened with a joke, how about repeating it with a different punch line?

    If you opened with a quotation, how about ending with the line that follows it?

    If you opened with a remarkable fact, what if you project that into the future?

Using the Word Bait you developed by answering these questions, you should now have establised the structure of your speech, including an outline with a beginning, middle, and end. Now, go back to your original Word Bait, answering, machines, and <u>me</u>, and spend another 15 minutes fishing for more associated words—metaphors—to help bring your speech to life. Like this:

ANSWERING	MACHINES	ME
guessing game	cause and effect	late
paternity test	relationship	office
research	competitive edge	sleep
reality check	the military	spouse
site inspection	accident	dogs
test	design	house
20/20 hindsight	precision	friends
accuracy	science fiction	clothes
evidence	specifications	tennis
firsthand account	theory	
hypothesis	trade secret	
password	field test	
proof	know which button	
trick questions	to push	
the whole truth	malfunction	

With this fresh bait, follow your speech's outline and spend the next 20 minutes writing "Answering Machines and Me."

TEN

Sock Hop:
Developing Names
and Advertising
Campaigns

SEAS
Compare
Socks with Insect
↓
Dirty ↔ *Insect*

TIDE POOLS
Varieties/Examples
ant
spider
scavenger
bedbug
flea
fly

Things/Places
carpet
kitchen
closet
aerosol spray

skin

corpse

Abstractions/Intangibles

speed

noise

color

Activities/Events/Processes

camping

disaster

gardening

Descriptors

repugnant

flea infested

His first morning meeting over, Aaron Kozak returned to his office a little before ten, looked toward the bay and instantly saw one of the Captain's Bait Buckets taped to the window. "Right on time as always," thought the Advertising Director. He walked over to the window, pushed it open and pulled in the note. Attached to the backside was an envelope. Aaron turned around to his desk, picked up his phone, and dialed an extension. "Jack?"

"Yo!"

"Round up Monty. The Great Outdoor Apparel Company is about to develop a name and ad campaign for its new insect repellent socks!"

"We'll see ya in five, boss."

Aaron put down the receiver and opened the envelope. The Captain had included a second sheet, but it was only an outline:

SEAS
Compare
Socks with Insects
↓   ↓
Shoes ↔ Camping
TIDE POOLS

Things/Places

_____

_____

_____

Abstractions/Intangibles

_____

_____

_____

_____

Verbs

_____

_____

Descriptors

_____

_____

_____

He got the hint. Aaron and his team were to fill up this second Bait Bucket on their own.

*   *   *

The Great Outdoor Apparel Company had put all of its hopes on breaking the summer sales slowdown with its new sock product. Thanks to the Captain's guidance, Aaron, his copywriter Jack, and graphic artist Monty had become expert fishermen. But this project required something extra, something special.

Earlier that morning, as he crossed the Village courtyard on his way to work, Aaron found his friend on a stepladder in front of The Treasure Chest, replacing the jewelry shop's awning. While the Captain continued working, Aaron told him about the new socks and how important it was to create just the right name and ad theme. "So, I thought maybe you could help us do some big game fishing," said the Advertising Director.

"And just how is young Lenny faring?" asked the Captain.

"Lenny? Lenny's fine," said Aaron, somewhat impatiently. He's . . . Well, in fact he was part of the team that came up with the insect repellent socks and . . . Hey . . . *You* were in that meeting, weren't you? I should have known that!"

Holding a corner of the awning's frame against the wall, the Captain turned to Aaron and winked. "Wrench, please."

Aaron began to rummage around the toolbox sitting beside a huge clay pot of wild flowers. "Is there anything around here you don't know about?" he asked, handing the Captain the wrench.

"Oh, my goodness, I should say so," said the Captain, as he began to hammer a nail into place with the wrench's flat face.

Aaron looked on, bewildered. "Ah . . . don't you think that a hammer might be more appropriate?"

Completing his task, the Captain turned back to Aaron. "Most certainly. However, as you might have noticed, a hammer is missing from this toolbox. So, rather than waste time searching for another one, I simply compared the attributes of a hammer with the remaining tools and came to the conclusion that the wrench would do quite nicely."

"You mean you *associated* the hammer with the wrench."

"In a manner of speaking. However, in order to associate the concept of a hammer with that of a wrench, I had to compare their attributes first—see what the two had in common. It's the same thing you did a moment ago."

"A moment ago I handed you the wrench."

Aaron started to help the Captain pick up the roll of new awning material. "Then, it was the moment before you so brilliantly assisted me with the wrench," said the Captain, eyeing Aaron with a grin.

He looked at the Captain. "The moment before that we were talking about Lenny."

"Exactly." The Captain pointed to the awning. "Your end please, Aaron."

"Oh, yeah," said Aaron, picking up his end of the awning again.

The Captain started back up the ladder. "You see, a moment ago you took the concept of <u>my</u> <u>asking</u> how <u>Lenny</u> was faring and *compared* that with the concept of <u>developing</u> the <u>insect</u> <u>repellent</u> <u>socks</u>. More precisely, you mentally listed a few of the attributes of both concepts, and compared the attributes themselves. Under <u>my</u> <u>asking</u> about <u>Lenny</u> you listed the <u>Captain</u> because in order to have asked about Lenny, I must have met him, and you listed the fact that he was in the new product <u>meeting</u> when the <u>socks</u> were created. Then, under <u>developing</u> <u>insect</u> <u>repellent</u> <u>socks</u> you listed the <u>Captain</u> and <u>meeting</u>, as you know my penchant for attending such gatherings. Comparing these lists of attributes, you discovered that what they had in common was the <u>Captain</u> and <u>meeting</u>. So in this instance, my friend, what you landed was **me**, or rather the concept that I was in that new product **meeting**. Hence your comment, 'You were in that meeting.' "

"I didn't even know I did that. I didn't know I compared anything."

"That's how the mind works. Comparing and associating concepts, ideas, and words—automatically. When you do that, all kinds of new possibilities open up. Comparing doubles your brain power. If you want to enhance your next fishing expedition, I suggest you begin by *comparing* Word Bait."

Giving the awning a shove that tossed it across the frame, Aaron gasped, "But how?"

"How do we always start fishing for new concepts?" asked the Captain, unfurling the material.

"With Word Bait from the problem."

"Which, in this instance, is . . . ?"

Aaron shrugged his shoulders. "The problem is naming insect repellent socks, so the Word Bait would be insect and socks. That part's easy enough."

"Splendid," said the Captain, as he prepared to move the step ladder to the other side of the frame. "Let's start with socks. Choose one attribute of socks."

Reaching up to tug the awning's ruffle into place, Aaron answered, "They're dirty."

"Exactly! And, given the hierarchies of Associational Thinking, what did you just do?"

"I expanded the initial Word Bait of socks into dirty. Now what?"

The Captain stepped off the ladder and straightened his blue paisley suspenders. "Take the concept of dirty and compare it with the concept of insect. What do they have in common?"

"You mean dirty socks?"

"No, just compare dirty, which is an attribute of socks, with insect."

He mulled the Captain's request over for a moment. "Gardening!"

"That's it, Aaron! That is just what comparing does. From either dirty or insect alone you might not have thought of gardening, but when you compared them, you arrived at that entirely new concept quite easily." As he finished lacing the awning to its frame, the Captain asked, "Do you remember the TIDE POOLS?"

"Sure. They're the last categories in the hierarchy that our mind uses to store information." Aaron paused. "And gardening would go in the Activities/Events TIDE POOL."

The Captain put the step ladder's loop handle over his shoulder. "Exactly. However, there are more attributes of socks than just their being dirty. If you were to continue the process, filling up a separate hierarchy for socks and dirty, eventually you would have two lists. Then you would compare the attributes on those two lists with one another, selecting the words that are common to each, thereby creating a new Bait Bucket of *compared* Word Bait. And it would be a very high powered Bait Bucket indeed! Likewise, you could start with simply dirty, an attribute of socks, fill up its hierarchy and then compare that with a hierarchy for insect, or a hierarchy from an attribute of insect such as camping."

Aaron handed the Captain the toolbox. "This sounds great. But, just in case I haven't got this compare thing down entirely, how about joining us for our meeting at ten?"

"I shall be there one way or another, my friend!" said the Captain.

∗   ∗   ∗

By the time Jack and Monty arrived for the meeting, Aaron had made two copies of the Captain's Bait Buckets. He told them how the Captain explained that comparing Word Bait was another super way to attract a Big Idea, and he showed them the Captain's filled-in Bait Bucket.

"Hey, this is a snap," said Monty after reviewing the Captain's list. "Ya just take dirty, compare it with insect and come up with a variety or example like flea. Which is definitely both dirty and an insect."

Looking at the Things/Places TIDE POOL, Jack added, "Yeah, and don't you just hate it when they leave their little corpses in the carpet?"

Monty sat up. "Why, we should add insect tombstones under Abstractions/Intangibles!"

The Great Outdoor Apparel Company's version of the Hardy Boys Plus One was off on another adventure.

"Well done, Monty," said Jack.

"I only follow your lead, word master."

Aaron pointed to the Captain's second sheet. "Now that we're all in the appropriate creative mood, the Captain has challenged us to fill up our own Bait Bucket with comparisons between shoes and camping. Let's start with the Things/Places TIDE POOL. We're looking for some things or places that have shoes and camping in common. Jack, as you are the appointed word master, your job will be that of the keeper of the Bait Bucket."

"I am up to it, sir!" said Jack, snapping open his notebook.

Monty crossed his arms and stared at his accomplice. "Aaron's always liked you best, Jack."

Aaron cleared his throat. "Gentlemen, begin!"

Studying his No. 2 pencil, Monty announced, "Boot camp."

"Works for me," said Jack.

"Then write it down, Bait Boy. Write it down!"

Jack obliged, putting boot camp under Things/Places.

"Rope," said Aaron.

"Rope?"

"Hey, this is Things/Places with shoes and camping. You need a rope for rock climbing, and you need special shoes," said Aaron.

Jack began to add it to the category when he stopped and looked at his fishing buddies. "Boys," he said solemnly. "I think we all ought to be sent to our beds without supper."

"Huh?"

"How could we possibly have missed the most obvious of all? Hiking boots!"

Aaron hung his head in mock shame. He stared at the carpet. He stared at his sandals. He stared at his toes. And then he simply said, "Snow shoes."

"Velcro," shouted Jack.

"And pebbles in your shoe."

"Blisters."

"Sporting goods and climbing boots. Hey, that oughta count for two. Or, is it four?"

Suddenly, Aaron raised his hand. "Time's up! Let's move to the next TIDE POOL category, Abstractions/Intangibles."

Monty hollered out, "Height."

Jack countered with, "Weight."

And Jack added, "Safety."

Next was the Verb TIDE POOL.

Silence surrounded the room. Coaxing them on, Aaron said, "Remember, we're talking about verbs in common with shoes and camping."

Jack pushed back his chair and began to pace the office.

"Dead give away, Jack," said Monty. "Now you have to add walk to the list."

"And while I'm doing that, I'll add slip and protect too!"

"They don't call you the word meister for nothing," said Aaron, who suggested that they move to Activities/Events. "And, I'll add the first piece of Word Bait. Hiking."

Monty winced. "Pain."

"Sick."

Jack and Monty stopped. "Sick?"

"Sick," answered Aaron. "Without shoes you could get into poison ivy, get insect bites, or all sorts of things. Lots of people get sick camping, you know."

"I know I got sick of it," added Monty, who began to mutter something about Yosemite's kamikaze squirrels.

"Okay, guys," said Aaron. "It's time for our Bait Boy to tell us what we've got so far."

In one mockingly elegant motion, Jack grabbed his notebook and stood up. "According to the official minutes of the meeting, thus far we have thus." He read off the categories with their pieces of bait:

TIDE POOLS

Things/Places
boot camp
rope
hiking boots
snow shoes
velcro
pebble in your shoe
blister

Abstractions/Intangibles
height
weight
safety

Verbs
walk
slip
protect

Activities/Events
hiking
pain
sick

Aaron rubbed his hands together. "Ready to go fishing for the big stuff, boys? Thanks to the Captain's new technique, we have *two* Bait Buckets full of freshly compared Word Bait. One with dirty and insect, and the other with shoes and camping. With this high-powered bait, our job of developing a name and ad theme for the insect repellent socks should be as easy as an overhead cast. Let's take the Captain's list first, starting at the top, with ant. Shout 'em out boys."

"Ain't no ant what can't be gone," said Jack.

"Hey . . . spider. We could have a **spider falling off its web** for a logo."

Looking at the list, Jack said, "Scavenger."

"My last girlfriend."

"Oou! And you really thought her name was Grace! Amazing, Aaron, truly amazing."

"Bedbug," said Jack.

"I got it. **Bugless Socks.**"

"Let's cast again."

"Closet. Hey, like mothballs, these could **keep bugs out of clothes drawers.**"

"Speaking of corpses, how about a visual of **dead bugs lying over a sock?**"

"Skin, could be **SecondSkin**. You know, like an extra layer of protection."

Monty looked at the first two pieces of Word Bait in the Activities/Events/Processes TIDE POOL. "Camping and disaster— now there's a natural combination."

Jack reversed his pacing pattern. "Why don't we give our list a try?"

They turned to their Bait Bucket of newly compared Word Bait. And even though Jack had wanted **CampNoItchyNoMore**, boot camp became **CampSocks**. Pebble in your shoe and rope gave Monty the idea of an ad with **a sock stepping down on an insect** and a **rock climber trying to scratch his ankle**. Under Abstractions/Intangibles, the team reeled in **WalkSafes** from safety, while **WalkSock**, **WalkLongs**, and **WalkAlongs** swam their way in from walk in the Verb category. In the Activities/Events TIDE POOL, Aaron hooked **HighHikers** from hiking.

Jack put all of their Catch onto a new sheet of paper he entitled Idea Creel:

spider falling off its web	**rock climber**
bugless socks	**trying to**
keep bugs out of clothes	**scratch his**
drawers	**ankle**
dead bugs lying over a sock	**WalkSafes**
SecondSkin	**WalkSock**
CampSocks	**WalkLongs**
sock stepping down on	**WalkAlongs**
an insect	**HighHikers**

Within minutes the new insect repellent socks were named **HighHikers**. Their logo became **a spider falling off its web**, and it was decided that their ads would depict people in a variety of outdoor activities, the first of which would be **a rock climber reaching down to scratch his ankle**.

While Monty and Jack were busy collecting papers and congratulating one another, Aaron looked out his window and watched a helix of seagulls effortlessly riding the air currents. "You know," he said, "this was a breeze. I don't know why I was so worried about it."

"The only trick is knowing where to cast, boss," said Jack. "After that, it's all in the wrist."

Word Bait Lesson No. 8

First you learned about Word Bait: What it is, where it is, and how to use it. Then you saw how to use the hierarchy and increase your fishing ability eight times over with the TIDE POOLS. Now, by comparing the hierarchies of two pieces of Word Bait with one another, your ability to develop new ideas will increase sixteenfold because you'll be using the full power of the hierarchy! Consider this:

Are franchising, real estate sales, burgers, and drive-throughs Big Ideas? You bet! But when the attributes of franchising were compared to those of real estate sales the result was Century 21 Real Estate Corporation. When the attributes of burgers were compared with those of drive-throughs the result was McDonald's. That's the power of fishing with compared Word Bait—entire industries can be transformed.

Comparing Word Bait doubles your brain power and it works just as well for any problem you're trying to solve. Even if it's writing a headline for a story about the similarities of people eating fish—and fish eating fish!

In that instance, you'd want all of the attributes, Word Bait, you could think of that are associated with the SEAS of Eating and Fish. After filling a separate Bait Bucket with the hierarchical TIDE POOLS for Eating and Fish, compare the two lists and create a third Bait Bucket with the compared attributes of each. Like this:

1.	2.
SEAS	SEAS
Eating	Fish

TIDE POOLS	TIDE POOLS

Things/Places	Things/Places
appetizer	catch of the day
cookbook	fish eye lens
water	bait
sushi bar	water
delicacy	coral reef
catch of the day	clam chowder
bakeware	

Abstractions/Intangibles	Abstractions/Intangibles
lunch hour	herringbone pattern
weight	fish story
craving	amount
amount	color
color	weight

Verbs	Verbs
propose a toast	bite
carve a turkey	marinate
bite	smell
brush after every meal	rise to the surface
compliment the cook	dart

Activities/Events	Activities/Events
room service	grunion hunting
bake off	canning
feeding frenzy	low tide
after dinner speech	feeding frenzy
cocktail party	

Descriptors	Descriptors
hungry	neither fish nor fowl
stuffed	slipper
salty	stuffed
al dente	big
halfbaked	fresh
easy as pie	underwater

Matching the two Bait Buckets creates a compared Word Bait
Bucket. Like this:

SEAS

Compare

<u>Eating</u> with <u>Fish</u>

Things/Places

<u>water</u>

<u>appetizer</u>

<u>bait</u>

Abstractions/Intangibles

<u>color</u>

<u>weight</u>

<u>amount</u>

<u>taste</u>

Verbs

<u>smell</u>

<u>bite</u>

Activities/Events/Processes

<u>feeding</u> <u>frenzy</u>

Descriptors

<u>stuffed</u>

<u>pickled</u>

Casting lines into these TIDE POOLS might hook such headlines
as: **Feeding Frenzy at the Shrimp Bowl, Lured to the Table,
Stuffed Pompano,** or **A Bite of Bait**!

Hook, Line & Sinker

Two different fishermen, two different kinds of Bait:

As a designer, Thom Bluemel markets his line of Rip Off tee-shirts primarily to teenage boys. In a world where "bad" means "good," Thom finds that the best shirt concepts come from comparing Word Bait. "I compared <u>sports</u> with <u>fire</u> and came up with **Speed Greed**." In addition to slogans, he uses this process to come up with graphic ideas. "I compared <u>skateboard</u> with <u>surfboard</u>, and got **bodyboard**. Then, I went back to <u>skateboard</u> and got **wheels**, **sidewalk**, and **asphalt**, all of which are part of the bodyboard tee-shirt background. It couldn't be easier."

*   *   *

After wading in for the first time, Jules DeSimone, of the Jules DeSimone Advertising Agency in Glen Mills, Pennsylvania, exclaimed, "This is like having an incredible idea factory at my fingertips!" His staff was on a tight deadline to produce a new summertime ad for a toy retailing client. "Just comparing <u>summer</u> with <u>animals</u> gave us more than enough concepts to complete the headline and body copy for the client's stuffed toy line ad in record time."

Word Bait Exercise No. 8

Remember the new car seat cushion that was developed in the Exercise in Chapter Three? Well, it's been officially named the Comfort-Ride. Now's the time to put what you just learned to work by creating a headline for the Comfort-Ride's first ad. Follow the lesson above and take 15 minutes to fill up one Bait

Bucket with TIDE POOL categories for <u>comfort</u>, and another one for <u>car</u>. Pull together the words that are in common with each list and you'll have your compared Bait Bucket. With your compared Word Bait, spend another 15 minutes going after your Big Idea. For a little help with this exercise, you may choose to refer to the <u>comfort</u> and <u>car</u> Bait Buckets listed in Part 4: Fishing Tackle.

The Catch

E L E V E N

Shipp Shape:
Modify and Evaluate

It was September 9, 1961, at 1:35 p.m. when senior classman Zack Shipp strolled into Mr. Ballard's Woodworking 101 class at Bay City High and laid his eyes on freshman Alfred Woodrow for the first time.

"This goofy looking kid holding this goofy little triangular piece of wood was just sitting there." Zack would usually let out a belly laugh at this part of the story. "But you know, he was holding it upside down, and I just knew by looking at Alfie's face that he had something special in mind. And that's how the 'A' and 'Z' of A to Z Shelves, Inc. first met—as God is my witness." In retelling the historic minutiae of the most successful furniture manufacturer in town, Zack would always pause at this point, just a count or two, so his listener could appropriately marvel aloud at the sublime coincidence that some call fate.

"Then, we met up again in 1980 at a Bay City High football game. Well, by then my little furniture plant was doing okay—and Alfie, he was a crackerjack carpenter. So we got to talking and I said to him, 'Alfie, whatever happened to that goofy upside down triangle shelf of yours?' 'Well,' he said, 'I figured it out!' So the very next day I saw one he'd built and the very next day after that, we went into business together!" Pause . . . one . . . two.

A born salesman, Zack could spread pleasure better than a John Deere. "Ain't no sense in leaving all your goodies in just one place," he'd say. Zack had been the one-man marketing and sales force behind A to Z's initial growth. His "aw shucks" attitude could disarm the most intransigent furniture store owner into finding display space for the triangle shelf. But the true genius behind the company was Alfred.

A quiet, steady, methodical sort who preferred a slide rule to a calculator and his wife's homemade soup to any "fancy restaurant-made food," Alfred had the physical stature and mental acumen of a "nerd" long before anyone knew the meaning of the word. The mere suggestion that he should give a speech to his several hundred employees at the company's plant unbalanced his physical processes to no end. However, Alfred was *more* than capable when it came to inventing things. He discovered how ceramic wall magnets, matching those in an inverted triangle shelf, could hold the shelf upright. Then he invented the formula for a humidity resistant, washable glue that would harmlessly allow a magnet to be attached to, and detached from, a wall. And then, he invented a release device that would free the wall magnets from the shelf magnets. As a result, A to Z Shelves, Inc. had been awarded a number of patents and lots of breathing room from any competition.

They had christened their product The Pyramid. As a large solid piece, apparently suspended on the wall, it would stand with its point on the floor. As a smaller piece, hung picture level, it would appear to float. Alfred and Zack sold them in chrome. They sold them in brass. They sold them in glass for office and home. And, they sold so many that their plant was in full operation 24 hours a day.

Then the Pyramid business turned upside down. Sales started to ebb like the tide. One month sales would be fairly good, and the next month they would drop by 15 percent, 20 percent, or more. Alfie had tried to bring this problem to his partner's attention. But when he sensed bad news heading his way, Zack would always duck.

"Hey, so it's Christmas time. Everybody knows that nobody buys much furniture at Christmas time. Right, Alfie?"

"Hmm."

"Hey, so it's the end of summer. Everybody knows nobody buys much furniture the end of summer. Right, Alfie?"

The pattern continued.

Finally, Alfred was able to sit Zack down and discuss the situation. He pointed his slide rule at the past twelve months' sales figures spread across the drafting table. "If our numbers keep going like this, nobody will be buying our furniture at any time of the year. I think we have to face facts, Zack, we need to come up with a new product, and fast, or we'll go under."

"Aw shucks, Alfie, all we really gotta do is some new ads. Or, maybe an infomercial or something. Hey, that's it! I'll be the host and we'll get some happy users to yap about how great their own Pyramid is."

"Zack, we've doubled our ad budget and gone into direct mail, but nothing is working. It's time to admit that The Pyramid is dying. We need something *new* or A to Z Shelves will be extinct in six months."

The edges of reality tugged at the back of Zack's mind and he didn't like it one bit. "You really mean it, don't you, Alfie? This is serious."

"Yes, Zack, I really mean it and this is serious. We're going to have to find a way to top the Pyramid shelf."

Reality had a stranglehold on him. "I'm going for a walk Alfred." His partner had hit home. That was Zack's stock response to serious trouble.

"Okay," said Alfred turning back to his drafting table.

Zack left the office and headed for the elevator. Remembering it was out of order, he changed direction and reached the stairway door just as it was closing. He walked into the dimly lit stairwell in time to see a familiar shape turn the corner of the platform below.

"Ahoy, Cap!"

The figure stopped his descent and called back, "Zack, would that be you?"

"Sure enough."

Reversing his direction, the Captain walked back up to greet his friend.

"Wonderful to see you taking the steps rather than the elevator, Zack. It is so very beneficial for your good health."

"Yeah, especially when the elevator doesn't work."

"To the contrary my friend, Federico had it up and running an hour ago. I assume you are off to another meeting with buyers?"

"Not exactly," said Zack, rubbing the back of his neck. "Say Cap, I'm mighty glad we ran into each other. Ya got a minute?"

"Why, of course," said the Captain. "How may I be of assistance?"

Zack told him that Pyramid sales were falling faster than the Hindenberg. "Alfie says we gotta get a *whole new* product but pronto, or we'll lose everything. I was just thinking maybe you could help come up with some new ideas like you did for that management problem we had awhile back."

"Why, I would be most happy to assist."

Moments later they entered Alfred's office.

Looking up from his sales figures, Alfred said, "Well, Captain, I was just about to go looking for you!"

As they greeted each other, the Captain said, "Zack has informed me that your Pyramid shelf may well become a thing of the past."

"The whole company may be, too, if we don't develop a new product that's successful," answered Alfred.

"Perhaps it isn't necessary to create an entirely new product," said the Captain. "There may well be aspects of The Pyramid that might be *modified* into a new, and as you say, Alfred, successful product."

"Modify? How on earth do we accomplish that?" asked Alfred, who had been set on developing an entirely new product.

"We can head for open water and your Big Idea by answering some Modify Questions. Using them as lures, these questions will put a new light on The Pyramid shelf, perhaps even bringing an entirely 'new' product to the surface. Your answers to these questions will give us just the bait we need to attract that Big Idea.''

"Shoot when ready, Captain," said Zack plopping himself down on the couch.

Alfred transformed his drafting table into a Bait Bucket easel by turning it to a vertical position and pinning large sheets of paper to it. Then the threesome began a question-and-answer session with the Captain leading the way.

The first thing he asked was, "What are all the components of your existing product? That will be the initial Word Bait."

"Well sir, we have shelving, an inverted triangle, and the wall space they attach to as components."

"Don't forget the magnets and washable glue, Zack."

"Right-O, Alfie!"

"What if any of these pieces of Word Bait could function alone or in a combination? Such as the magnets and the washable glue?"

"Gee, we could put those little suckers most anywhere, to hold just about anything to a wall."

"What if you place something that is normally on the bottom on the top, reversing positions?"

"Hey guys. Why not shelves, any kinda shelves, overhead? You know, like up near the ceiling?"

"The shelves could run the distance of a wall," added Alfie, turning around in his drafting chair to write down the answer.

"What if you make appearance less important?" asked the Captain.

"Airplanes," said Alfred raising the black marker as if to help make his point. "Those overhead storage bins in airplanes don't take up any additional space. They're functional, and you don't really see them when they're closed."

"You're suggesting we go into the airplane business, Alfie?"

"No, not at all. I'm saying that we could use the magnets to run a **storage unit**, with the same design as those airline storage bins, **close to the ceiling**, along one wall."

Zack perked up. "By golly that's a crackerjack idea!"

"Now," said the Captain, "what if that appearance were changed superficially, or perhaps cosmetically?"

Zack's eyebrows knitted together. "We could paint 'em."

"We could," added his partner, "make the units so our buyers could paint them any color they wanted. That way they could blend into existing decor or even be painted an accent color."

Zack slapped both hands on his knees and declared, "Why, Alfie, that's how come we're partners. You got brains, kid!"

The Captain continued. "And, what if it appealed to different age or social groups?"

"Kids," announced Zack. "We could make these things in psychedelic colors, and kids would think they're real cool."

Leaning back, the Captain thought for a moment. "Perhaps it would even make cleaning their rooms more appealing."

Alfred turned around from his drafting table, faced his two companions with a grin, and proclaimed, "College kids! There's never enough storage space in dorm rooms."

Nearly bouncing off the couch, Zack let out a holler. "We got our first market for our new storage unit! Keep a-going, Cap."

Following Zack's direction, the Captain asked, "How might your new storage unit appear if you looked at it through a piece of colored glass?"

"Well," said Alfred. "We might consider upholstering it."

"This thing has decorator item written all over it," said Zack with a laugh. Alfred turned to write decorator item down.

"What if certain materials maintained their own identities?"

Looking at the back of Alfred's head, Zack said, "We could sell the magnets and glue so people could use 'em for their own custom shelves. Right, Alfie?" Alfred's head nodded as he wrote down Zack's answer.

"What if you changed the shape?"

"Change the shape? Hey, Captain, we got a good deal here—let's not go messing with it."

"Wait a minute, Zack. Why couldn't we change the shape? Right now we have a storage bin in a semicircle shape running the length of a wall and attached at either end by our magnets. Why not change that semicircle shape into a . . . **star shape?**"

"Why, Alfie! That's—"

Even the Captain found himself caught up in the joy of discovery. "Splendid, Alfred, simply splendid! Now, what if you softened something?"

"Soft makes me think of frilly, like some ruffle thing or something. Hey, how about a kinda ruffle or something? A kinda **wall accent like crown molding**, but this could be any material somebody'd want, and it could be wrapped around a rod that's held up by our magnets."

"Why, Zack, I'm proud of you," said Alfred.

"What about joining forces with another group?"

"You know, we could use this idea for **drapery** or even **shower curtain rods**!" Empowered by his own fishing ability, Zack continued, "Sure as shooting, some drapery manufacturer's gonna love this idea. It'd give 'em a whole new product. Hey, Alfie, we could just license this thing out and retire in cash cow city!"

"Why, Zack, I am *really* proud of you."

"What is the most unusual arrangement you can think of for the magnet and glue?" the Captain asked.

"Slap it on the ceiling," said Zack.

"Slap it on the ceiling, attach a wide tube of light cloth down to the floor, and put a light in it," countered Alfred. Then he slowly turned toward their guest and quietly said, "Captain, I think we've just invented a new form of **tube lighting**."

"Yes, indeed you have, my friend."

"Holy cash cow, Alfie!"

"What if you combined different functions such as a sofabed or a clock radio?" continued the Captain. His question was instantly met with a silence of the purest form. "Then again, perhaps it would be best to review the Word Bait that we began with," suggested the Captain.

"Inverted triangle . . . magnet . . . washable glue . . . shelf . . . wall. Inverted triangle . . . magnet. Magnet. . . inverted triangle. Inverted triangle *with* a magnet." Alfred was fishing in uncharted waters, but something kept pulling his line. With a few short strokes of his marker, he wrote in big, bold, black letters, **Bed Frame**.

"Wow!" said Zack envisioning a bed being held up by a wide, low, inverted triangle. "That there is a real conversation piece."

"What other arrangements can you think of for inverted triangle?"

"Use it for the **base of a dining room table—**"

"A **coffee table—**"

"—or, even **end tables**, Alfie!"

Next, the Captain asked, "What is the most unusual arrangement you can think of for washable glue alone?"

Zack sat back. "Shoot, glue is glue. It could be used most anywhere," said Zack.

"What if you place something back-to-back?"

Alfred finished writing down washable glue, turned around and said, "It could be used to **hang pictures** on the wall."

"Apartment owners are gonna just *love* this."

"Or **wallpaper**," continued Alfred. "Or even **wall mirrors**."

"What could you learn by building a working, scale model of your idea?"

"Hey, Alfie, this would be great for the **arts** and **crafts market**. Shoot, this would be great for the mass market."

Alfie swiveled toward his easel.

"What if you change an identity?"

"Well," said Alfred, "we could make one version for **home use**, one for **school use,** and one for **industrial use!**"

The partners shook their heads in disbelief that they had been able to modify their Pyramid shelf into so many new product ideas in such a short time. Thinking the meeting had come to an end, they got up to thank their friend.

"Oh, heavens no," said the Captain, raising his hands in protest. "Our work is merely half complete. Now that we have effectively modified your shelf and reeled in some excellent Big Ideas, we must still evaluate your Catch."

"Evaluate?" said Zack. "Why these ideas are just fine the way they are. Like I said before, Captain, let's not go messing with a good idea."

"Wait a minute, Zack. The Captain's got a point. How else will we know if any of these ideas are really keepers?"

"Why, you got yourself a point there, Alfie."

They sat back down and Alfred made a list of all the great ideas they'd hooked:

> Overhead storage units, designed like those in airplanes
>
> Overhead storage units, designed like a star
>
> A rod that would be covered by different types of material and act as a wall accent like crown molding
>
> Drapery rods
>
> Shower curtain rods
>
> Tube lighting hanging from the ceiling
>
> Use the inverted triangle shape for bed frames
>
> Use the inverted triangle shape as the base for dining room tables
>
> Use the inverted triangle shape as the base for coffee tables
>
> Use the inverted triangle shape as the base for end tables
>
> Use the glue to hang pictures
>
> Use the glue to hang wallpaper
>
> Use the glue to hold wall mirrors up
>
> Package the glue for the arts and crafts industry
>
> Package the glue for home use, school use, and industrial use

"Which shall we begin with?" asked the Captain.

"The crown molding one," volunteered Zack.

"Then that it is, my friend," said the Captain. "Our current purpose," he said in a cautioning tone, "is to *evaluate* your Catch. The best way to do that is with Evaluate Questions, which will help us take a good look at it, scale it, filet it, and determine whether or not we think other people will like it enough to buy it. In the event Word Bait surfaces during this process, Alfred, you should by all means write it down. However, our real goal is to size up your Catch to see whether or not it's worth keeping."

Alfred nodded.

"Fire at will, Cap."

He began, "Is your concept of a crown molding replacement easy to understand?"

"Piece of cake, Cap."

"How easy is it to explain to others? Could you explain it in twenty-five words or less?"

"Zack, the Captain's right. We can't keep calling it the crown molding replacement. It leaves too much to the imagination."

"How about custom wall accents?" Zack suggested. "Or, reusable wall accents?"

Alfred frowned a little and wrote the names down. "You're getting closer."

"How easy is the product to use?"

"Easy as pie," said Zack. "We could make the pole adjustable to fit odd length walls. All you'd have to do is put fabric over it like a sock, bunch it up for that ruffle kinda look, and snap the pole against the wall magnets."

"Will it make something easier to do or simpler to use?"

Alfred took a turn. "Well, once you put crown molding in, it stays there. However, this product would be very easy to detach, so you could take it with you every time you moved."

"On a scale of one to ten, how original, how novel, how fresh is the concept?"

"We're talking twelve."

"Are you fully aware of what appeals to this marketplace?"

"I think we'll have to rely on our years in the furniture business," answered Alfred.

"How might you make this concept more appealing?"

"We would be able to, say, take a piece of material that matches a customer's sofa, and produce a matching ruffle. Or, we could have a variation of materials, colors, and patterns. Perhaps even stars and stripes like your suspenders, Captain."

"Why, in that event, I would be most flattered."

"Next question, my Captain," said Zack.

"What are the major strengths of your concept?"

Alfred offered an answer. "It's easily interchangeable and portable."

"What are the major weaknesses of your concept?"

Alfred eyed the hardwood floor and then his partner. "You know, Zack, this could be done without our magnets."

"Don't sweat it, Alfie. Without our glue, they'd leave a mess on the wall, and they'd have to buy new parts to move the sucker."

"Realistically, what evidence do you have that this concept will succeed?"

Zack ducked. "Aw, shoot, we know a good thing when we see it, Captain."

"We haven't done any market research on this, Zack. We just came up with the idea 10 minutes ago."

"Who else could give valid advice about this concept's feasibility and implementation?"

Alfred was ready for this one. "We could do some testing with a local department store—set up a kiosk and have a questionnaire for people to fill out."

"Is the customer willing to pay the asking price?"

"Odds are, this thing could be real cheap. It'd beat the pants off crown molding."

"Speaking of pricing," said the Captain, "how does the concept lend itself to adaptation for other markets, such as people with higher incomes?"

"We could change materials again," said Alfie. "Maybe even something like a long cube of marble-looking material that the rod runs through."

"What spin-offs does this concept suggest?"

"Easy. We'd sell all kinds of material that'd cover the rod."

"What subgoals does this give you?"

"We gotta get between the sheets with some big manufacturer. Maybe a big drapery or decorating company."

"Imagine yourself in the future looking back on your current decisions. What would you think you did right?"

Zack Shipp stood up, looked at his two friends and announced, "We fished real good!"

The Catch Lesson No. 1

Believe it or not, lots of good folks fall in love with their Big Idea. But before they can turn that Big Idea into a Great Idea, they must take two last steps. Modify it and evaluate it.

Like Zack, you might say, "Let's not go messing with a good idea." It's your idea and it's great. While you subjectively fished for that super concept, now you must objectively review it. To see if it needs fine-tuning or if it can be expanded, apply the Modify Questions and then follow up with Evaluate Questions. If your Catch can't stand up to this type of review, you'd better throw it back.

In this context, Modify becomes much more than a garden-variety verb. It's part of the process that may lead to a transformation of your basic idea or to a radically different understanding of the problem altogether. If Nobel Prize winners James D. Watson and Francis Crick hadn't flip-flopped (modified) their double helix model, the structure of DNA might still be a mystery.

Then, the last step, in a linear sense, is to evaluate your Catch before you start bragging about it. Is it feasible? Is it practical? Is it original? Is it effective? Think of the Evaluate Questions as a reality test that you can actually apply as a course correction maneuver in either the beginning or the middle of this process but always at the end of it.

Hook, Line & Sinker

Astute anglers can save money and become more effective:

When Canada's PanCanadian Petroleum Company needed to develop new concepts to advance the use of their technology, they turned to Lance Secretan of The Thaler Corporation, who worked with 30 technological specialists to fish for them. According to Lance, thousands of oil well heads in Alberta are shut down for three weeks of every year in order to clean and maintain them. PanCanadian's production would fall about 11,000 gallons per well head during this time. How could they keep the oil flowing while they completed the maintenance? "We fished around <u>oil</u> and <u>flow</u> and hooked onto the idea of **renting tanker cars** that could be filled while the well head on the pump was serviced." All told, the new concepts that the group generated will add approximately $200,000,000 to PanCanadian's profit line.

*   *   *

After writing a speech he's planning to give to his Board of Trustees, John Slorp, president of the Minneapolis College of Art & Design in Minneapolis, Minnesota, then puts it to a real test—he runs it through the Evaluation Questions, answering each as if he were a member of the Board. According to John, knowing how someone might perceive the presentation helps him create one that will really be effective.

The Catch Exercise No. 1

You finally bought that watch company you'd been eyeing. You've "right-sized" the employee pool, beefed up the ad budget, and installed new manufacturing equipment. But sales have run aground. It's time to fish or cut bait and sell your collective assets. You decide to fish. And you do so by modifying your existing series of fine watches.

The watch components, Word Bait, you'll be working with include:

numerals   watchcase
watch stem   clock works (movement)
clock hands   mainspring
watch face   battery
watchband   gems

Select as many pieces of Word Bait as you like. For the next 20 minutes attach them to the following Modify Questions and see what swims your way. Perhaps it will be a line of watches for children, a his and hers set, or a waterproof sports timepiece with a built-in stop watch.

1. What if you make the appearance more important than the quality?

2. What if you were to change the character of a physical sensation?

3. What if you were to change a different visual quality, such as a partial view?

4. What if you linked different sensations such as color-shape or color-sound?

5. What if its appearance were to symbolize something?

6. What if its appearance mimicked something else?

7. What if it appealed to a different social group such as conservative or avante-garde?

8. What if you make it more expensive or extravagant?

9. What if its features were surprising?

10. What if its appearances were deceiving, like an optical illusion or a mirage?

11. What if its appearance were variable as in a change of costumes or wigs?

12. What if its appearance were to alter with the passage of time such as in the changing of the seasons?

13. What if it were quickly to change form?

14. What if it were to switch identities back and forth?

15. What if its appearance were distorted?

16. How would it appear through a filter?

17. What if you change the size?

18. What if you change the shape?

19. What if you change the texture?

20. What if you use the analogy of a fashion collection?

21. What if a temperature change were to affect the appearance?

22. What if it looked more high tech?

23. What if it looked simpler or less intimidating?

24. What if you express an idea more graphically?

25. What if you caricaturize a person?

26. What is the most surprising or outrageous way in which you could modify the physical appearance?

27. What if you simply combine one or more current purposes?

28. What if you combine different functions as in a body part with more than one function?

29. What if you borrow features of two or more categories of products and services, like combining tools into a Swiss army knife?

30. What if some parts were interchangeable?

31. What if you were to design a single piece to take the place of several?

32. What if you borrow principles or processes from another discipline such as archaeology or detective work?

33. What if you bring about visual harmony?

34. What if all or part of it were a rendition of a basic shape such as a diamond?

35. If it's two-dimensional, could you make it three-dimensional or make it appear three-dimensional?

36. What if you could provide it in assorted shapes?

37. What if it were twisted, braided, or intertwined?

38. What if it were angled or sharply bent?

39. What shape would it be if you flipped it over?

40. What if it could change identity by assuming different shapes such as a Transformer toy?

41. What if it were to lose its shape?

42. What if the texture were changed?

43. What if it were distorted?

Now that you've enticed your big Catch on board, it's time to evaluate it. If you've fallen in love with your own idea, you'll never be able to filet it when necessary so that you can serve it up. Remember, this step is not for the squeamish fisher. You'll have to take a good look at it, weigh it, and in some instances clean and gut it.

For the next 20 minutes, with your Catch in mind, answer the following Evaluate Questions. If you discover your Big Idea stinks, throw it out!

1. What difficulties do you foresee in putting your idea into practice?

2. Who else could give valid advice about feasibility and implementation?

3. If you think your goal is not attainable as stated, what would be a satisfactory alternative?

4. What spin-offs does your idea already suggest?

5. How does it lend itself to adaptation for other audiences, such as older people, younger people, or people of the opposite sex?

6. What parts of your idea can be used to solve other problems?

7. What if you were to field-test a prototype or a working model of your idea?

8. What are the major strengths of your idea?

9. What are the major weaknesses of your idea?

10. On a scale of one to ten, how original, how novel, how fresh is your idea?

11. Has something like this existed before?

12. How is this version more suitable for the times?

13. Which of the following groups of positive descriptors could a critic apply to your idea, and why?

    intriguing, absorbing, engrossing, gripping, fascinating
    stimulating, stirring, awakening, piquing, provocative
    thrilling, electrifying
    spirited, animated, sparkly, spunky, zestful, lively, bright
    palatable, appetizing
    tangy, spicy, fiery, peppery, savory, gingerly
    amusing, diverting, entertaining
    learned, erudite, informative, well-informed
    inspiring, enlightening, visionary
    significant, important, monumental
    relevant, helpful

14. Which of the following groups of negative descriptors could a critic apply to your idea, and why?

    insipid, bland, mild, blank; no personality
    vapid, stale, flat, lifeless; no spirit, sparkle, or tang
    barren, arid, meager, unable to satisfy the
        hunger of the mind
    banal, tasteless, trivial, platitudinous, truistic

ordinary, obvious, pedestrian, uninspired
wishy-washy, limp-wristed, weak, diluted
inane, purposeless, pointless, devoid of significance
stupid, asinine, unintelligent
irksome, tiresome, wearisome
dull, humdrum, dreary, monotonous, repetitive
pedantic, heavy, stodgy, bookish, overly exacting
slow, plodding
irrelevant; unhelpful

15. Is your idea similar to something else?

16. How closely have you met the criteria of an "elegant" idea?

    Is it precise?
    Is it neat?
    Is it simple?
    Does the idea "feel right"?

17. How easy is your idea to understand?

18. Does your idea improve ease of maintenance?

19. How does your idea affect someone's quality of life?

    How does it affect safety?
    How does it affect physical comfort?

20. What overt or subtle stereotypes are embodied in your idea, such as that of highly educated people?

T W E L V E

Bouillabaisse:
A Fisher's Final
Thoughts

*"All achievements, all earned riches,
have their beginning in an idea."*
—Napoleon Hill
author of *Think & Grow Rich*

Dear Friend,

By now you have learned that the human mind stores information, concepts, in a way that's as logical and organized as the structure of the atom or the galaxies that wheel invisibly through the nighttime sky. Simply by using the principle of Associational Thinking you may gain rapid access to the limitless possibilities locked within your memories—and, better yet, specialized talents or creative genius isn't required to do so.

I encourage you to go fishing for Word Bait whenever you're trying to solve a problem or create a new idea. Depending upon the amount of time you have, and whichever is the easiest for you, use the Six Universal Questions, visualization, the hierarchy of OCEANS, SEAS, and TIDE POOLS, or the compare technique. Should you be stymied from the very beginning, answer a few of

Defining the Problem Questions first. And when you have hauled in your Big Idea, finish up with the Modify and Evaluate Questions.

By following the guidelines in this book, you'll be able to convert your memory into solutions to deal with problems and discover new ideas you never thought possible. Truthfully, this ability is already in your mind. However, now it is at your command to use whenever you want, for you have just discovered how to be consistently creative!

The time has come for you to go fishing on your own. Bait your hook with some initial Word Bait, cast your line to bring in even bigger Word Bait and go after the Big Ideas. Clean them. And filet them. Then throw them in a big pot and cook up a bouillabaisse stew. Somewhere in there will most certainly be a winner!

Good Luck!

The Captain

P A R T   4

Fishing Tackle

Bait Buckets

Have you run out of Word Bait to develop a new <u>comfort</u> feature for a <u>car</u> in the Chapter Three Exercise or to write that new product's headline for the Exercise in Chapter Ten? Well, you'll find plenty here! The following 23 pages are brimming with just the Word Bait you're looking for. Imagine what other new ideas you can create just by reading through them.

COMFORT

Varieties/Examples

adjustable
air-conditioned
balmy (mild/pleasant)
barefoot
brisk (cool/bracing)
comfortable as a pair of
    old shoes
cool as a cucumber
cozy
cushioned
down-home
homey
luxurious
on easy street
peaceful
restful
snug as a bug in a rug
soothing
spacious
toasty
warm and cozy
well-off

People/Animals

butler
flight attendant
host
hostess
maitre d'
millionaire
mother
personal attendant
purser
steward (caretaker/
    manager)

Things/Places

adjustable bed
adjustable headrest
after-sun lotion
air mattress
air-conditioner
air-conditioning
airplane seat
analgesic (pain relieving
    drug)
analgesic rub
antacid
apartment

armchair
armrest
backrest
back scratcher
balans chair
balm
bare feet
bathrobe
beanbag chair
bed
bedrest (cushioned back
    with arms)
bedroom slippers
belt
bench seating
berth (sleeping space)
bleachers
bolster
booth (seating)
bow stabilizer
box spring
breathing (woven) T-shirt
bucket seat
bus seat
Cadillac
calamine lotion

camper (truck)
carpet
carpet padding
car-seat cushion
central air-conditioning
central heating
chair (piece of furniture)
chair back
clothing
coat and tie
cocktail lounge
Coleman heater
comforter
comfort station
conversation pit
costume
cotton (fabric)
couch
creature comforts
cruise ship
cushion (pillow/soft pad)
den (room)
desk chair
dolman sleeves
down comforter
down pillow
down sleeping bag
Dramamine
dressing gown
easy chair
elastic (stretchable
    material)
elastic hosiery
electric blanket
electric socks
father's chair
favorite chair
feet
fiberfill
fireside
flannel nightgown
flat heels
flexible watchband
foam rubber
foot massager (roller/
    electric)
footstool
furniture
garment vent
hammock
hand fan

hand warmer
hassock
headrest
heated garage
heated pool
heater
heating pad
Hide-A-Bed
home
hospital bed
hot compress
hotel bed
hot-water bottle
housecoat
housedress
house slippers
innerspring mattress
Jacuzzi (whirlpool bath)
jumpsuit
king-size bed
kneeling pads
lamb's wool
lamb's-wool mattress pad
leather/plastic seat when
    hot/cold
lice (body and head)
limousine
living room
lounge for first-class
    passengers
lounge furniture
loungewear
low heels
luxury car
mattress
medication
moccasins
modesty panel (on office
    desk)
mother's arms
mountain cabin
nightshirt
nose pads on eyeglasses
nurse's shoes
padding (cushioning)
pajamas
pantyhose
passenger ship
passenger train
passenger van
pencil gripper

penthouse
pillion (passenger saddle)
pillow
pressurized cabin
protective padding
Pullman car
recliner chair
resort
riding lawn mower
rocking chair
rollaway bed
Rolls Royce
room
running shoes
running shorts
saddle
saddle blanket
saddle pad
satin sheets
seat (chair/place to sit)
seat cover
seat cushion
sedative
seersucker
seersucker suit
sheepskin car-seat cover
shock absorber
shoe insoles (removable)
silk sheets
sleeping car
sleepwear
slippers
sneakers
soft-soled shoes
spacecraft capsule
space suit
sponge rubber
sport shirt
sportswear
stagecoach
stand-up desk
straight chair
sweat suit
swimsuit
teachers' lounge
teddy bear
telephone shoulder rest
tennis shoes
theater seat
thermostat

throw pillow
toilet seat
travel accommodations
tuxedo
underwear
vibrating bed
vibrating chair
VIP box
VIP lounge
walking shoes
walking shorts
washboard road
water bed

Abstractions/Intangibles

bed of roses (luxurious situation)
breathing space
cabin pressure
cost
decor
doctor-patient relationship
effect of temperature
elbowroom (adequate space)
ergonomics (human engineering)
facial expression
headroom (amount of space)
heat (warmth/form of energy)
interior design
legroom (amount of space)
luxury
passenger comfort
peace and quiet
peace of mind
physical condition
position
prosperity
relative humidity
security
standard of living
status quo
style (trend/fashion)
sympathy
temperature
vision (sense of sight)
voice of a loved one
wealth

Verbs

acclimate
adjust the thermostat
blow on your hands
breathe easily or freely
comfort (console/soothe)
crawl into a person's lap
cuddle
curl up by the fire
eat crackers in bed
fall asleep in your chair
feather your nest
kick off your shoes
kneel
loosen
lower or raise the seat
move to another seat
plug your ears with your fingers
pressurize
put your feet on the furniture
recline
reveal your feelings
roll down the window
rub an itch
scratch an itch
settle down with a good book
shade (verb)
share a bed
shift position
shift weight
shift weight from foot to foot
sit
sit by the fire
sit on a person's lap
sit on the floor
sit with feet tucked under
sit with foot placed on knee
sit with your feet on the desk
sleep
sleep during a plane flight
sleep in lover's arms
slip between the sheets
slip into something comfortable
soak in the tub

soak your feet
soothe
sprawl out
stroke (touch/caress gently)
suck your thumb
take off your shoes
ventilate
warm the bed

Activities/Events/Processes

back rub
breakfast in bed
camping trip
cozy fire
fair weather
flying
foot massage
massage (activity)
pain control
restful sleep
rubdown
sitz bath
smooth landing
smooth ride
temperature control

Descriptors

at home
baggy
beltless
comfortable dry (vs. wet)
elastic (stretch, return to shape)
familiar
first-class
fluffy
half-sitting, half-reclining
hard (firm)
heated
hot (temperature)
informal
king-size
loose
overstuffed
quiet
satiated
simple (plain)
soft
uncrowded

Pontiac
Pontiac Bonneville
Pontiac Firebird
Pontiac Grand Prix
Pontiac Trans Am
Porsche
presidential limousine
propane-powered auto
racecar
Rambler
rear-engine automobile
red sports car
Renault
rental car
roadster
robotic car
rocket car
Rolls Royce
Saab
sedan
Shirley Muldowney's pink
    dragster
slot car (miniature racing
    car)
soapbox car
solar-powered car
speedster (roadster)
sports car
squad car
staff car
stalled car
Stanley Steamer (steam-
    powered car)
station wagon
steam-driven auto
stock car (race car)
stolen car
stretch limousine
Studebaker
Studebaker Hawk
stunt car
Stutz Bearcat
Subaru
subcompact car
Suzuki Samurai
taxicab
touring car
town car
toy car
Toyota
Toyota Corolla

Triumph (automobile)
unmarked car
used car
vintage automobile
Volkswagen Beetle (Bug)
Volkswagen Rabbit
Volvo
woody (station wagon)
Yellow Cab
Yugo

Varieties/Examples
(trucks/buses/vans)

18-wheeler
1-ton truck
3/4-ton truck
airport shuttle
armored car
articulated bus
automobile transporter
beer truck
Bigfoot (truck)
Black Maria paddy wagon
bloodmobile
bookmobile
bread truck
Brink's armored truck
cab-over-engine truck
camper (truck)
cargo van
catering truck
cattle truck
cement truck
Chevrolet Astro Van
Chevrolet El Camino
Chevrolet Luv
city bus
crash truck (arprt
    emrgncy vehicle)
cross-country bus
delivery truck
delivery van
diesel truck
Dodge Caravan (van)
dump truck
express bus
fire engine (pumper)
fire engine (pumper-
    ladder)
fire engine with elevating
    platform

flatbed truck (lowboy)
Ford Aerostar (van)
Ford Ranger (truck)
four-wheel-drive vehicle
fuel truck
garbage truck
gasoline truck
GMC Safari (van)
Good Humor truck
Greyhound bus
hand truck
hook-and-ladder truck
hotel shuttle
ice-cream truck
jitney
kneeling bus (for easy
    access)
Land Rover
livestock truck
logging truck
London double-decker bus
lumber truck
lunch wagon
Mack truck
mail truck
milk truck
minibus
Mitsubishi Wagon (van)
mobile concession stand
monster truck
motor coach (bus)
motor home
moving van
Nissan Van
omnibus (public vehicle)
panel truck
passenger van
patrol wagon
Peterbilt (truck)
Philippine jeepney
pickup truck
pickup truck with full
    gun rack
Plymouth Voyager (van)
police van
Popemobile
prison truck
recreational vehicle
repair truck
rolling stock (company's
    vehicles)

RV (recreational vehicle)
school bus
shuttle bus
side loader (delivery truck)
sound truck
sport truck (customized vehicle)
street sweeper (cleaning vehicle)
tank truck
Tonka Truck toy
tour bus
Toyota Van
toy truck
trolley bus (trackless trolley)
TV news van
UPS truck
van
Volkswagen Vanagon
water truck (dust-control vehicle)
water wagon (drinkng water carrier)
wheelchair-accessible bus
wheelchair-accessible van
Winnebago
wrecker (tow truck)

Varieties/Examples
(trailers)
2-wheeled trailer
4-wheeled trailer
boat trailer
bus trailer
camper (trailer)
double-wide mobile home
flatbed trailer
horse trailer
livestock trailer
mobile home
pig (piggyback, RR to tractor)
reefer (refrigerator truck)
semitrailer
tent trailer
tractor-trailer (semi)
trailer for hauling goods or animls
U-Haul trailer or truck
utility trailer

Varieties/Examples
(motorcycles/motorbikes/ ATVs)

3-wheeler (ATV)
4-wheeler (ATV)
bicycle with a motor
BMW (motorcycle)
BSA (motorcycle)
chopper (motorcycle)
Ducati (motorcycle)
electric 3-wheeler
Harley-Davidson (motorcycle)
hog (Harley-Davidson nickname)
Honda (motorcycle)
Honda Transalp (motorcycle)
Katana (motorcycle)
Kawasaki Ninja (motorcycle)
minibike
moped (motorbike)
motorbike
motorcycle
motorcycle with sidecar
motor scooter
Norton (motorcycle)
police motorcycle
street bike
Suzuki (motorcycle)
swamp buggy (ATV)
trail bike
Triumph (motorcycle)
Yamaha (motorcycle)

Varieties/Examples
(miscellaneous vehicles)

amphibious cargo carrier
amphibious landing craft
amphibious tractor
amphibious vehicle
armored personnel carrier
ATV (all-terrain vehicle)
backhoe
ball collector (golf course vehicle)
Batmobile
bulldozer
cab-over-engine tractor
carryall (earth mover)

Caterpillar tractor
cherry picker (passenger crane)
corn picker
cotton picker
cultivator
drilling rig
earth mover (scraper)
electric cart
Explorer wheelchair
forklift
GPV (gravity-powered vehicle)
gypsy caravan
half-track (military vehicle)
harvester
hydraulic excavator
log lifter (skidder)
military Jeep
military vehicle
missile launcher
mobile crane
off-road vehicle (ORV)
power shovel
reconnaissance vehicle
riding lawn mower
road grader
rocket launcher
self-propelled combine
simulator (experimental model)
skatemobile
skid loader
snowmobile
snowplow (snow-clearing vehicle)
snow tractor
steam-powered tractor
steamroller (road roller)
tank (vehicle)
toy tractor
tractor
tractor-mower
troop truck
wheelchair (hand-driven/ motorized)
wheel loader
wrecking crane
Zamboni ice resurfacer

Varieties/Examples
(drivers)

backseat driver
bus driver
cabdriver
camel driver
child behind the wheel
cross-country driver
dogsled driver
driver (vehicle operator)
drunk driver
getaway driver
good driver
hit-and-run driver
hotdogger
hot-rodder
low rider (customized-car
  driver)
motorcyclist
motorist
New York cabbie
pedicab driver
poor driver
racecar driver
reckless driver
road hog
show-off
slave driver
slowpoke
speed demon
speeder
stagecoach driver
stock-car driver
student driver
stunt driver
sulky driver
Sunday driver
test driver
truck driver

Varieties/Examples
(traffic signs)

Bus Stop (sign)
Caution: Student Driver
  (sign)
Children At Play (sign)
Dead End (sign)
Deer Crossing (sign)
Do Not Back Up! Severe
  Tire Damage
Do Not Enter (sign)

For Sale (sign)
international road signs
Just Married! (sign)
Lane Closed (sign)
Loading Zone (sign)
Narrow Bridge (sign)
No Honking (sign)
No Left Turn (sign)
No Outlet (sign)
No Parking (sign)
No Passing (sign)
No Riders (sign)
No Right Turn on Red
  (sign)
No Thoroughfare (sign)
No Thru Street (sign)
No Trucks (sign)
No U-Turn (sign)
No Vehicles Allowed
  (sign)
Ped Xing (sign)
road sign
School Zone (sign)
Slippery When Wet (sign)
Soft Shoulder (sign)
speed limit sign
Stop (sign)
stop sign
street sign
traffic-conditions sign
traffic sign
Watch for Falling Rocks
  (sign)
Wide Load (sign)
Wrong Way (sign)
Yield (sign)

Varieties/Examples
(supplies/equipment)

antifreeze
anti-icer (device or
  additive)
automotive jack
Auto Shade (folding
  windshld shade)
booster cable
brake fluid
car alarm system
car mat
car-seat cushion
car stereo

car vacuum
car wax
CB radio (citizens band)
cellular telephone
coolant
diesel fuel
fabric protectant
fender skirt
fiberglass
first-aid kit
fish-eye mirror
flare (signal light)
flashlight
floor jack
floor mat
fuel
gasohol
gasoline
gear (paraphernalia)
grease (oily substance/
  lubricant)
gun rack
infant car seat
leaded gasoline
license plate bracket
license plate sticker
litter bag
low-octane gasoline
lubricant
luggage rack
lug wrench
mobile telephone
motorcycle helmet
mud flap (splash guard)
oil (viscous substance)
outside car mirror
pickup crossbed tool box
plug-in spotlight
premium gasoline
radar detector
regular gasoline
Revenger (fake weapon
  on car dshbd)
road flare
seat cover
sheepskin car-seat cover
side-view mirror
siren (warning device)
spare tire
spotlight
squeegee

stereo sound system
tape deck
taximeter
tire chains
tire iron
tire pressure gauge
tire pump (foot-operated)
tire pump (hand-operated)
tool kit
towing bar
towline
trailer hitch
transmission fluid
truck bed liner
unleaded gasoline
visor mirror
window covering

People/Animals

accident victim
Andretti, Mario
aristocrat
auto mechanic
automotive engineer
auto worker
backyard mechanic
beginner
Benz, Karl
bootlegger
border patrol
bus conductor
car buff
car dealer
carhop
car pool
car salesperson
car thief
celebrity
chauffeur
child
Chrysler, Walter
collector (hobbyist)
commuter
daredevil (reckless
    person)
delivery person
De Lorean, John
designer
dog
doorman
driving instructor

Ford, Henry
Foyt, A. J.
garbage collector
gas line (waiting line at
    gas station)
Good Humor man
grease monkey
Guthrie, Janet
Hell's Angels
highway patrol
hitchhiker
homeless family living
    in a car
Iacocca, Lee
independent trucker
James Bond (007)
kidnapper
kidnap victim
Knievel, Evel
long-distance trucker
mail carrier
mechanic
meter maid
milkman
Moss, Sterling
mother
motorcycle escort
motorcycle gang
motorcycle passenger
Mr. Goodwrench
Mr. Magoo
Muldowney, Shirley
    (ChaCha)
Oldfield, Barney
old person
owner
parking attendant
parking meter monitor
Parks, Rosa
passenger
pedestrian
Petty, Richard
pit crew
police escort
police officer
Porsche, Ferdinand
proud new owner
race crew
repo man
Sales, Soupy (Milton
    Hines)

school crossing guard
service station attendant
shade-tree mechanic
smokey (highway patrol)
smuggler
Stewart, Jackie
teenager
tour guide
tourist
traffic cop
traffic violator
transit commission
traveler
traveling salesman
Unser, Al
Unser, Bobby
used-car salesman
VIP (very important
    person)
Yarborough, Cale
yuppie

Things/Places

advertisement
air pollution
airport parking
alley
assembly line
assembly plant
attached garage
autobahn
automobile junkyard (car
    graveyard)
automobile museum
automobile pollution
automobile safety-check
    sticker
Automotive News
    (magazine)
avenue
award for safe driving
back road
barrier
    (fence/obstruction)
belt highway (beltway)
bicycle
bicycle lane
bicycle lock
bird droppings
blind curve
blind spot

blizzard survival kit
blocked lane
blue book (NADA vehicle
  value book)
boarding area
body shop
Bonneville Salt Flats
border crossing
bottleneck
bridge (road span)
broken glass on the road
bumper sticker
bus depot
bus lane
bus pass
bus route
bus station
bus stop
bus ticket
campground
canvas water bag
car
Car and Driver (magazine)
caravan (vehicles traveling
  togther)
carbecue (car crusher)
car beverage holder
car bomb (bomb set to
  car ignition)
carbon monoxide
car coat
car cover
car key
car pool lane
carport
cartop boat
car-wash brush
car-wash facility
car window tray at
  drive-in restaurant
cat's paw tracks on a car
  hood
center lane
certificate of registration
chauffeur's license
chock (wedge/block)
chop shop (illegal
  auto-parts shop)
circular driveway
circus caravan
citation (summons)

city
city map
city street
claim check
cloverleaf (highway
  interchange)
coasting hill
cobblestone street
collision-damage waiver
  (CDW)
computer
Consumer Reports
  (magazine)
convoy
country road
crash dummy
creeper (wheeled
  platform)
crossroads
crosswalk
curb (concrete edging of
  street)
darkness
Daytona Int'l Speedway
dead animal on a highway
dead battery
dead man's curve
deathtrap
decal
dent (small hollow/
  depression)
Denver boot (car
  immobilizer)
desert (arid region)
destination and distance
  sign
detached garage
detour (alternate route)
Detroit, MI
diesel smoke
dip in the road
directional arrow
direction sign
dirt road
downtown
downtown parking
drag strip
drip pan
drive-in church
drive-in movie

drive-in restaurant with
  carhops
drive-in window
driver's license
driver's manual
driveway
driveway blocked by
  bikes and toys
driving gloves
driving school
driving simulator
emergency lane
emission
exhaust fumes
express lane on highway
expressway
eyeglasses
farm
fast lane
ferryboat
flashing green light
flashing red light
flashing yellow light
flatcar auto rack
fleet of vehicles
food
foot-operated air pump
four-way stop
freeway
freeway exit
fuzzy dice hanging from
  car mirror
garage (repair shop)
garage (vehicle shelter)
gas can
gas pump
gas-tank key
gift
glare of headlights
golf course
gravel road
grease gun
grease rack (hoist)
green light
grocery cart
guest parking
hail damage
hairpin curve
hands
hand signal

Harrah's Automobile
Collection
head injury
heated garage
Henry Ford Museum
high school
highway
highway interchange
highway mirage
hill
home
homestretch
horsedrawn carriage
hydraulic jack
hydraulic lift
icy highway
icy street or road
ignition key
import item
impound lot
injury
inside lane
intersection
interstate highway
itinerary
junkyard (scrapyard)
lane
learners permit
left lane
license
license plate
lighting
lights from oncoming
traffic
line of taxis
loading dock
loading zone
log (record)
logo
Los Angeles, CA
lovers' lane
luggage
magnetic car sign
magnetic key case
main drag
main road
main street
maintenance contract
map
merging lane
miniature (scale model)

mobile home park
model (prototype)
moisture in the fuel line
motel
motorcycle driver's
license
motorcycle jacket
motor pool
Motor Trend (magazine)
motor vehicle
Motown (Detroit
nickname)
mountain pass
mud
Nat'l Motor Museum
neutral (gear position)
newspaper's auto section
New York, NY
next year's model
nonskid surface
off-ramp
one for the road
one-way street
outside lane
overpass
owner's manual
parade float
park (gear position)
parking garage
parking lot
parking meter
parking space
parking space for the
disabled
parking sticker
parking stripe
parking ticket
passing lane
passing zone
payload
pedestrian crossing
pedicab
police checkpoint
police radar gun for speed
detection
pothole
power source
proof of insurance
public transportation
racetrack
radar trap

railroad crossing
rain (precipitation)
refrigerated freight
container
regular route
rent-a-car booth
Rent-A-Wreck
replica
reserved parking
residential area
resident parking
rest area
restricted lane
ricksha
right lane
Road and Track
(magazine)
road barrier (temporary
barricade)
roadblock
road hazard
road map
road salt
road shoulder
roadside stand
road tunnel
road washed away
route
Route 66
rust (coating formed by
oxidation)
safety sticker
salesroom
salvage yard
scale model
scarf
scenic lookout
S curve
serve-yourself gas pump
service contract
service entrance
service record
service station
service station restroom
showroom
sidewalk
signpost
skid marks
skyway (elevated
highway)
slippery highway

slipstream (suction behind vehicle)
slow lane
slow vehicle
slushy roadway
smog
snack (light meal)
snow (ice crystals)
solid line on highway
Southern California
speed bump
speeding ticket
speed shop (hot-rod garage)
speed trap
status symbol
steep road
stoplight
straightaway (straight stretch)
street
street markings
stripes on highway or road
suburb
suction-cup animal on car window
sunglasses
switchback road
taxi stand
test track
thoroughfare
thruway
timetable
tire tracks
title (certificate of ownership)
token
Tokyo
tollbooth
toll bridge
tollgate
toll road
tool
tow-away zone
toy (plaything)
trade-in
traffic circle
traffic cone
traffic light (traffic signal)

traffic ticket (traffic citation)
trail (path/track)
Trans-Amazon Highway
Trans-Canada Highway
transfer ticket
transportation terminal
travel accommodations
truck-driving school
truck farm (truck garden)
truckload
truck route
truck stop
tunnel (underground passage)
turnaround (space)
turning lane
turnout (passing space/ track)
turnpike
two-way street
underground parking lot
underwater tunnel
used-car lot
vanity license plate
vehicle weight scale
visitor parking area
warehouse
washboard road
wayside park or rest area
wheelchair ramp
whiplash injury
windshield sticker
written warranty
yellow caution light

Parts
(cars/trucks/motorcycles)

4-cylinder engine
6-cylinder engine
8-cylinder engine
accelerator (speed control device)
afterburner (on engine)
air bag
air brake
air cleaner
air horn
air vent
alternator

aluminum (common metal)
ammeter (ampmeter)
antenna (aerial)
antenna flag
antenna in windshield
antipollution device
antismog device
armrest
ashtray
automatic choke
automatic seat belt
automatic transmission
automobile engine
automobile seat
automobile upholstery
axle
back of the bus (segregated area)
backseat
backup light (vehicle backing light)
battery
bellows (bus-trailer connection)
bench seating
bias-ply tire
brake (slowing or stopping device)
brake drum
brake lights
brake lining
bucket seat
bumper
bunk (sleeping place)
cab (on truck/heavy equipment)
cable
car air-conditioner
car ashtray
car bumper
carburetor
car defroster
car door
car grille
car heater
car radio
car tailfin
car trunk
car windows frosted inside

catalytic converter
chassis
child's car seat
chrome trim
cigarette lighter
  (automotive)
clearance lights on
  vehicle
clutch (transmission
  device)
column gearshift
computerized fuel system
console (unit)
container chassis
Continental kit (spare-tire
  holder)
convertible top
courtesy light
crankshaft
cruise control (mph
  control setter)
curb feelers
curtain
custom body
cylinder (engine part)
dashboard
dashboard light
deadman brake
decorated rear window of
  vehicle
decoration
  (ornamentation)
defogger
diesel engine
differential gear
digital lock
dimmer switch
dipstick
disc brake
distributor (engine
  device)
dome light
door
door handle
door lock
driveline of vehicle
drive shaft
dry clutch
electronic instrument
emergency brake
emergency light

emergency vehicle light
emission control
engine
exhaust manifold
exhaust muffler
fabric
fan belt
fender
fender flag
fins
first gear (low)
flashing lights
flat tire
floor
floorboard
floor covering
flywheel
fogged windshield
fog lights
fold-down seat
foot pedal
fourth gear
frame (skeleton)
friction brake
friction clutch
friction drive
front seat
front-wheel brakes
front-wheel drive
frosty car window
fuel gauge
fuel-injection system
fuel line
fuel pump
fuel tank
gas cap
gas pedal
gas tank
gauge (measuring device)
gear (mechanism)
gearbox
gearshift
glass (material)
glove compartment
hand brake
hand crank
headlight
headlight beam (high/
  low)
headrest

heater
high-performance engine
hood of an automobile
hood ornament
hood release
horn (sound maker)
hub
hubcap
hydraulic brake
hydraulic liftgate on
  vehicle
ignition
ignition lock
independent suspension
  system
inner tube
instrument panel
internal-combustion
  engine
jump seat (small folding
  seat)
knob
lap seatbelt
lavatory
leather
left-hand steering
lever
lift gate
lock (security device)
mag wheel
manual transmission
marque (auto nameplate
  or emblem)
material (raw material)
metal
methanol
Michelin tire
monster tire
motor
muffler (on engine)
odometer
oil filter
oil gauge
opaque glass
opera window in car
overdrive gear
overheat indicator
paint sealant
parking lights
passenger hand strap
personalized car paint job

pinstriping on automobile
pipe (tube)
plastics
police car light
power antenna
power brake
power door lock
power seat in a vehicle
power steering
power steering fluid
power window
privacy partition
pull cord
push button
quartz-iodine lamp
rack
rack-and-pinion gear
rack-and-pinion steering
radial tire
radiator (engine cooler)
radio (thing)
radio antenna
rear-view mirror
rebuilt part
recapped tire
reclining car seat
reflective glass
reflector
retread (tire)
reverse gear
roll bar
roof
rotary engine
rubber
rubber bumper
rumble seat
running board
rustproofing material
safety glass
seat (chair/place to sit)
seatbelt
second gear
shatterproof glass
shock absorber
shoulder belt (seatbelt)
signal light
sissy bar
snow tires
solenoid
speedometer

spoke wheel
spring (device)
sprocket wheel
standard transmission
starter (engine
    mechanism)
steam engine
steel
steel-belted tire
steering column
steering gear
steering wheel
stick shift
strut (brace)
sunroof (electric/manual)
sun visor
supercharger
sway bar (vehicle
    stabilizer bar)
tachometer
tail fin
tailgate
taillight
tail pipe
temperature gauge
thermostat
third gear
throttle (thing)
thrust bearing (absorbs
    end load)
tie rod (connecting brace)
tinted glass
tire
tire tread
tonneau (waterproof car
    covering)
torque converter in
    transmission
tow-truck sling
tow-truck wheel lift
transmission
trouble light
truck bed (standard/long)
turbocharger
turn signal
twin-cylinder engine
two-wheel drive
undercarriage
undercoating
universal joint
upholstery

vehicle's brake system
vehicle's cooling system
vehicle's electrical system
vehicle's fuel system
vehicle's steering system
vehicle's suspension
    system
vent
vinyl
vinyl top
warning light
water pump
wheel
wheel lock
wheel spokes
whitewall tire
window
windshield
windshield defroster
windshield washer
    control
windshield wiper
wiring
wobbly wheel
wood

Abstractions/Intangibles

adolescence
aerodynamics
affordability
age
American automobile
    industry
American obsession, an
automobile club
automobile industry
automobile loan
automotive engineering
auto parts business
average speed
bartender responsibility
    law
beeping sound
big business
Big Three auto makers
book value
business
bus line
busman's holiday
bus schedule
car alarm (sound)

car allowance
car insurance
car noise that can't be
  pinpointed
carrier (transportation
  line)
carrying capacity
car's collision rating
child's imitation of
  vehicle sound
chug of an engine (sound)
clanking sound
clean record
color
complexity
conditional warranty
convenience
cost
crunch or squeak of
  frozen snow
daily rate
dealership
depth perception
design (pattern/motif)
diesel fuel octane rating
direction
distance
down payment
drivability
driving ability
driving age
driving conditions (road
  cnditions)
emission standards
emotions (feelings)
engine rhythm
estimated damages
estimated time of arrival
  (ETA)
fare
finance charge
financing
fine (penalty)
fuel economy
fun
gas mileage
gasoline octane rating
gasoline tax
good deal
grade (slope)
hazard

headroom (amount of
  space)
height
highway fatality
  prediction
holiday schedule
horsepower
humming sound
hydraulics
image (popular
  conception)
installment plan
insurance
investment
Japanese automobile
  industry
job perk (perquisite)
joke about driving
knocking sound of engine
law (legislation/rule)
legroom (amount of
  space)
lemon law
length (linear
  measurement)
license number
load limit
luxury
maintenance cost
make and model
mandatory rest period
manufacturer
mechanics
memories
metric system
metropolitan bus line
mileage
mileage allowance
miles per hour (mph)
minimum age
model number
moment of impact
motor vehicle regulations
mover (van line)
music
nationwide bus line
new-car smell
New Year's Eve
night
night blindness
no-fault insurance

noise (sound)
noise pollution
number per population
ooga-ooga (horn sound)
ownership
parts guarantee
passenger comfort
payload capacity
payment
peripheral vision
pickup (acceleration)
pinging sound
pleasure
police siren (sound)
power (energy)
power (strength/force)
purr of an engine
putt-putt (engine sound)
rattling noise
rebate
registration number
resale value
rest stop
revolutions per minute
  (RPMs)
ridership
right-hand steering
right-of-way
roar of the engine (sound)
rules and regulations
rules of the road
rush hour
RV club
safety (security)
salability
sales tax
schedule
seatbelt law
security
senior citizen fare
sense of direction
serial number
shape (form/contour)
size
snail's pace
sound (audible noise)
sound of air brakes
sound of screeching
  brakes
sound of squealing tires

sound of vehicle's
  back-up beeper
speed (rate of motion/
  rapidity)
speed limit (maximum/
  minimum)
state department of motor
  vehicles
steam power
sticker price
stress (emotional strain/
  tension)
technology
temperature
the 1920s
the 1930s
the 1940s
the 1950s
time (period/duration)
toll (tax/charge)
top speed
total loss
traffic advisory
traffic code
traffic conditions
traffic court
traffic death toll
traffic noise
transit authority
transportation industry
transportation technology
travelers' advisory
  (weather info)
trucking company
trucking song
turning radius
value
vehicle number
vehicle weight tax
velocity
visibility
vision (sense of sight)
warning
warranty
weather advisory
weather forecast
weight
weight limit
West German automobile
  industry
wheelbase

width
winter

Verbs

abandon
accelerate
adjust the antenna
approach
arrest
arrive
ask directions
avoid
backfire (explode)
back into
back up (move backward)
beat the traffic
blare the horn
blare the radio
block (impede/hinder)
board (embark)
borrow
bounce
brake (slow down or
  stop)
break down (fail)
break the speed limit
buckle up
bump (collide with/hit)
burn rubber
buy
careen
carry (haul/transport)
catch a bus
catch a cab
change (make or become
  different)
change a flat tire
change direction
change lanes
change off (alternate)
change oil
change seats
charter (hire for
  temporary use)
chase (pursue)
chase cars
chauffeur the kids around
check the oil
check the tires
check under the hood
choke a motor

climb into
coast
collect
collide
come to a dead stop
commandeer
commute to work
couple (link/join)
crank the engine
crank up
crash (break/collide/
  collapse)
crash into a crowd
crash through a gate
cross an intersection
cross over the line
crowd off the road
cruise down the highway
crunch (chew or grind
  noisily)
crush (press/squeeze/
  crumple)
cut in
cut off
decelerate
decorate
delay
deliver
demolish
dent (make a dent in)
depart
depreciate in value
detach the odometer
detour (avoid by going
  around)
dicker (bargain)
die (expire)
dig out
dim the lights
direct traffic
disembark
disengage (release)
dodge
double-park
drive at dusk
drive at night
drive behind a truck in
  the rain
drive in fog
drive in reverse
drive in the city

drive off a bridge or ferry
drive off a cliff
drive on icy highway
drive through mud or snow
drive to and from work
drive with one hand
drive without lights
drive without thinking
drive wrong way on one-way street
eat at a drive-in
elude a pursuer
empty the ashtray
enjoy
enter a freeway
escape
escort
exit a freeway
explode
export
fall asleep at the wheel
fasten a seatbelt
ferry
fill
find a body in a car trunk
fishtail
fix (repair)
flood the engine
forget to fasten your seat belt
forget to put into park
forget to release parking brake
forget to turn off the lights
forget where you're parked
get an estimate
get a ticket
get into a car
get lost
get out of a car
give a person a lift
give directions
go around (avoid)
go forward & reverse to get unstuck
go on tour
go through a stop sign

grease (lubricate with grease)
grind the gears
grip (take firmly/hold fast)
grip the wheel
gun the engine
hail a cab
haul
haul away
haul freight
haul to market
hear
hire
hit (strike)
hit a bridge abutment
hit a bump
hit an animal
hit a tree
hit a vehicle broadside
hitchhike
hit the guard rail
hit the road
honk in a tunnel
honk the horn
hot-wire
hydroplane on pavement
idle the engine
import
impound
inspect
jaywalk
jump from a car
jump-start
jump the curb
keep air in the spare tire
kick the tires
learn to drive
lease (let or rent)
leave
lend
lift a car with your bare hands
live in a car
load (verb)
lock bumpers
lock gears
lock your keys in the car
look ahead
look both ways
look cool
look for a parking space

lose a wheel
lose control
lose speed on a hill
lose your keys
lose your license
lose your way
lower or raise the seat
lubricate
lurch forward
make a deal
make a mistake
maneuver
merge into traffic
misgauge the distance
miss a bus
miss an exit
miss a ride
move a house or building
navigate
obstruct
offer a ride
overcharge
overhaul
overheat
overload
oversteer
pack (load/stuff)
paint (verb)
park a vehicle
park illegally
pass another vehicle
pass a tractor-trailer (semi)
pass out at the wheel
pay attention
peel rubber
pick up a hitchhiker
plan (devise/prearrange)
plow into (ram)
polish (verb)
pollute
protect
pull (verb)
pull over
pump the brakes
push
push car seatback forward
push to start
put your shoulder to the wheel
race (go fast)

race a train
ram (drive into/hit violently)
rattle (shake noisily)
reach the end of the line
read a map
rebuild
recharge
recover a stolen vehicle
reduce speed
refuel
regulate
rent (verb)
rent a car
repaint
repair
replace
repossess

restore
restore to original condition
restrict automobile travel
reverse (verb)
rev up
ride (verb)
ride in a car
ride in a convertible
roar
roll (verb)
roll downhill
roll down the window
rotate the tires
run a red light
run down (knock down)
run out of gas
run over

rush (move with haste or eagerness)
sabotage
salvage
scrape (scratch/rub harshly)
screech
sell
shake
shift down
shift gears
shift up
shimmy
ship
shop around
sideswipe
signal (give a signal)

F O U R T E E N

SEAS

The Word Bait Exercise in Chapter Eight challenged you to develop concepts for <u>dog</u> <u>food</u> and television <u>commercials</u>. Sail through these SEAS and fill in their TIDE POOLS with even bigger Word Bait.

ability/skill/talent
accidents/disasters/survival/rescue
accurate/precise/correct
achievement/success/failure
action/motion/movement/rhythm
adolescence/stereotypes of teenagers
advice/exhortations/folk wisdom
Africa/people of Africa
age/young/old
aggressive/fierce/wild/uncivilized
agriculture/farming/ranching
airflow/wind/blow/fan
air/gases/vapors
Americana/Mom, baseball and apple pie
American politics/politicians/elections
amount/intensity/degree
amusement parks/fairs/carnivals/circuses
ancestry/heritage/genetics/evolution
ancient Egypt/ancient Greece/ancient
    Rome
anger/rage/resentment
archaeology/prehistory/ancient
    civilizations
architecture/architects
Arctic Regions/the Arctic/Antarctica
armed forces/military life
arrange/sort/classify
arrive/enter/exit/leave/return
art/artwork/artists
astronomy/spacecraft/space travel
Australia/New Zealand

authentic/artificial/true/false
automobiles/trucks/motor vehicles
balance/equilibrium
baseball/softball
basketball/basketball games
beaches/harbors/bays/ports
beauty/ugliness/attractive/unattractive
bend/fold
billiards/pool
bird/fowl
bit/lick/suck/chew/sting
black/gray
blue/purple
boating/watercraft
body fluids/bodily wastes
bones/muscles
books/publishing
bottom/below/down
boundaries/borders/edges
bowling/bowling alleys
brain/nervous system
bravery/courage/heroism
break/damage/destroy
breathe/choke/gag/suffocate
brown/tan
bubble/gurgle/fizz
buildings/construction
business/industry
California/Los Angeles/San Francisco
camping/hiking/mountaineering
Canada/Nova Scotia to British Columbia

Caribbean/Hawaii/South Pacific
carry/convey
celebrate/holidays/parties/parades
ceremonies/rituals
change/fluctuate/temporary
chase/pursue/capture/trap/escape
check/review/examine/inspect/detect
chemistry/chemical elements/com.
   materials
Christmas/New Year's/Hanukkah
circles/spheres/rings/ovals/loops
cities/towns/city life
clarify/understand
clay/concrete/plaster/cement/ceramics
cleaning/dirty/clean
clear/transparent/translucent/opaque
clothing/fashion/style
collection/gather/collections/museums
colors/colorful
comfort/discomfort
commercial transportation/ship/haul/
   deliver
common/familiar/ordinary/usual
compete/win/lose/awards/prizes
complain/find fault/criticize
compliment/admire/respect/honor
computers/software/robots
conceal/hide/lose
condense/contract/shrink
conformity/nonconformists/independence
confusion/chaos/disorder
conservation/ecology/the environment
containers/storage
continue/repeat
control/lack of control
controversy/debate/argue/disagree
cooking/eating/meals
copy/duplicate/imitate
cost/value/expensive/inexpensive
courteous/rude
covers/wraps/lids/caps
crime/criminals/murder/terrorism
cruelty/torture/brutality/savagery
curiosity/interest/boredom
curves/arches/concave/convex
cut/drill/grind/abrade/penetrate
cycles/bicycles/motorcycles
dance/dancers
Dark Ages/Middle Ages/Renaissance
day/daytime/morning/afternoon
death/dying/funerals/burials

decisions/choices/judgment
decor/decorating
decrease/reduce/subtract
depth/deep/shallow
designs/patterns/motifs
detach/release/unfasten
deteriorate/decay
difficult/hard to accomplish
dig/plow/bury
dishonest/disloyal/deceptive
dislike/avoid/annoy
disobedient/defiant/rebellious
distance/far/near/close by/remote
dogs/cats/family pets
doors/gates
drinking/beverages/liquor
driving/traffic
early/late/waiting
earthquakes/volcanoes/slides/avalanches
East Asia/Southeast Asia/South Asia
East. Europe/Russian Fed./former U.S.S.R.
easy/easily
efficient/convenient/timesaving
elevators/stairs/ladders
emotional healing/recovery
emotions/feelings
energy/electricity/fuels/nuclear power
engines/motors
espionage/spying
ethics/morality/right and wrong
excitement/thrills/adventure
expand/stretch/spread
exploration/discover/explorers
fabric/cloth/leather/fur
faces/facial expressions/heads
factories/manufacturing
fame/famous
family life/child rearing
fasteners/adhesives/fasten/attach
fear/phobias/cowardice
female/femininity/sex-role stereotypes
fict. characters/monsters/cartoons/comics
field sports/track and field/indoor sports
fighting/fighting sports
fill/empty
fire/burning/firefighting
fish/marine mammals/crustaceans
flat/level
float/sink
floors/floor coverings

flow/drip/flood/squirt/spray
flying/aircraft/air travel
food/food groups
football/football games
foreign governments/world leaders
forests/jungles/trees
formal education/schools/teachers/
    students
forward/backward/back and forth
friendship/kindness/friendly/congenial
fun/play/recreation
furniture/furnishings
gamble/bet
games/puzzles
generosity/altruism/giving/gifts
geo. features/mountains/wilderness/parks
glass/mirrors
gold/silver
golf/golf courses
greed/selfishness
green/greenish
grip/slip/slide/cling
grow/develop
guard/protect
habits/gestures/mannerisms/body language
hair/feathers/baldness
handwriting/typing/word processing
hang/suspend
happiness/laughter/smiles
hard/rigid/firm
hate/detest/abhor
headgear/masks/neckwear
health prob./illness/diseases/injuries/pain
health treatments/hospitals/caregivers
hearing/ears/sounds
heart/blood/organs/glands
heaven/hell/utopias
height/high/low/tall/short
help/aid/assist
history of the U.S./settlement to the
    present
hit/whip/collide/kick
hobbies/arts and crafts/handicrafts
holes/openings
honest/loyal/reliable/trustworthy
horses/horse. riding/horse-drawn
    vehicles
hoses/pipes/tubes
household appliances/kitchen appliances
houses/apartments/living quarters
human sexuality/sexual mores

humor/comedy
hunting/animal trapping/blood sports
ice hockey/ice hockey games
identifiers/nicknames/symbols/flags
imagination/creativity
inclined/sloped/oblique
income/wages
increase/enlarge/add on
infancy/childhood
information transfer/info. systems/
    libraries
insects/spiders/worms
inside/center/middle
instructions/orders/commands
insurance/insure
international relations/diplomacy
invest/investments
jewelry/gems
judiciary/legal systems/the courts
jump/bounce/deflect/reflect
kitchenware/pots and pans/dishes/
    glassware
knowledge/philosophy
labor relations/strikes/unions
landmarks/monuments/memorials
language/foreign languages
law enforcement/police
leadership/lead/follow
length (linear meas.)/long/short
lighting/light sources/shade/darkness
like/want/prefer
limbs/appendages
linens/bedding/towels
lines/linear/straight
liquids/semiliquids/gels
literature/writers
live events/spectator sports
loneliness/isolation/absence
loose/loosen/tight/tighten
loss/grief
love/romance/dating
lower/fall/drop
luggage/purses/wallets
magazines/periodicals
mail/letters/messages/postal service
maintenance/repair
male/masculinity/sex-role stereotypes
mammals/wild animals/domesticated
    animals
marketing/advertising/selling
marriage/weddings/divorce

measure/estimate/test
medical sci./med. research/human anatomy
meetings/conventions/conferences
memory/remember/forget/nostalgia
mental health/mental illness
messy/disorganized/untidy
metals/alloys
Mexico/Central America/South America
Middle East/Afghanistan to North Africa/Greece
Midwestern U.S./Midwest/Ohio to Dakotas
mistakes/incorrect/inaccurate/imprecise
mix/combine/combinations
money/banking/finance/economics
motionless/inactive/passive
motivation/energetic/lazy
mouth/teeth/dental care
movies/movie stars
music/musical instruments/musicians
mythology/legends
navigate/maps
negotiate/agree/agreements/contracts
new/modern/fresh
news/newspapers/TV and radio news
night/evening/nighttime
Northeastern U.S./East Coast/NYC/D.C.
Northwestern U.S./Oregon/Washington/ Alaska
numbers/counting
obedient/submissive/compliant/tame
obstacles/barriers/fences
occupations/jobs/work
oceans/tide pools/islands
offices/office environment/office supplies
official/unofficial/formal/informal
oils/fats/grease/lubricants
older adults/retire/old people stereotypes
Old West/Westward Expansion
open/close
opposite/contrary/reverse
optimism/pessimism/confidence/self-doubt
organizations/clubs
outdated/old-fashioned/obsolete/used/ stale
outside/front/back/sides
paper/cardboard
parapsych./astrology/superstition/magic/ luck

peace/harmony/relaxation/contentment
peoples/countries
permanent/stable/unchanging
personal grooming/cosmetics/toiletries
personality/personal relationships
photography/videotaping/photo production
physical fitness/exercise/nutrition/dieting
physics/mathematics
plan/predict/forecast/the future
plants/flowers/gardens/gardening
plastic/rubber/synthetic materials
political activism/militancy/social change
pollution/garbage/hazardous waste
popular songs/popular music/singers
posture/stand
poverty/poor/needy
pressure/press/squeeze/crush/crowd
prevent/limit/restrict
printing/printed materials/graphics/type
problem solving/problem solvers
pumping/suction/vacuum
punishment/penalties/prisons
push/pull/attract/repel
quality/standards/perfection
racing/races
radio/radio personalities
railroads/trains/rail systems/train travel
rain/snow/sleet/hail/fog
raise/lift/elevate
rank/grade/rate
rectangles/squares/triangles/polygons/ cubes
red/pink
religion/clergy/places of worship
remove/eliminate
reproduction/pregnancy/birth
reptiles/dinosaurs/snakes/amphibians
research/experiments/scientific method
restaurants/bars/nightclubs
rights/freedom/equality
rivers/streams/waterfalls/dams
rocks/stones/minerals/ores/mining
rods/poles/posts/cylinders/cones
rooms/kitchen/living rooms/bedrooms/ bath
rope/string/bands/straps/belts
royalty/aristocracy
rules and regulations/laws/codes
sadness/misery/regret/crying
safety/danger/risk

warm (temperature)

Miscellaneous

A man's home is his
castle.
At ease!
Make yourself
comfortable.
Pull up a seat.

CARS

Varieties/Examples

abandoned vehicle
Alfa Romeo
ambulance
American muscle car
antique car
Aston Martin
Audi
Avanti
Bentley
Blue Flame, The (rocket
car)
BMW (automobile)
brougham (car model)
bubble car
Bugatti
Buick
Buick Riviera
bulletproof car
Caddy (Cadillac
nickname)
Cadillac
Cadillac Eldorado
Chevrolet
Chevrolet Camaro
Chevrolet Chevette
Chevrolet Corvair
Chevrolet Corvette
Chevrolet Nova
Chevy (Chevrolet
nickname)
Chrysler
Chrysler Fifth Avenue
Chrysler New Yorker
Citroen
classic car
clunker (jalopy)
compact car
company car
convertible (car model)

Cord (automobile)
coupe
Daihatsu
Datsun
De Lorean (innovative
car)
demonstrator (sales demo
model)
De Soto
Dodge
dragster
driver-education car
Duesenberg
dune buggy
economy car
Edsel
electric car
Excalibur SS
experimental car
family car
fastback (car model)
Ferrari
Fiat
first car
floor model
Ford (automobile)
Ford Escort
Ford Model A
Ford Model T
Ford Mustang
Ford Pinto
Ford Taurus
Ford Thunderbird
foreign car
Formula 1 race car
front-engine automobile
funny car (at circus or car
event)
gas guzzler
getaway car
Golden Bugatti
golf cart
government fleet car
government limousine
hardtop (car model)
hatchback (car model)
hearse
Holden (Australian car)
Honda (automobile)
Honda Civic
horseless carriage

hot rod
Hot Wheels toy
Hudson (automobile)
Hyundai
Isuzu
Jaguar
jalopy
Jeep (AMC Jeep)
jet car
junker (dilapidated
vehicle)
kiddie car
Lamborghini
lemon (defective product)
limousine
Lincoln Continental
Lincoln Town Car
loaner (temporary
replacement)
Lotus (automobile)
low rider (customized
car)
lunar rover
luxury car
M.G.
mail Jeep
Mary Kay pink Cadillac
Maserati
Matchbox Car (toy)
Mazda
Mercedes Benz
midget racer
miniature car
Mitsubishi
model car (scale model)
model car (toy)
motorcar (automobile)
new car
Nissan
old car
Oldsmobile
Oldsmobile Delta 88
oncoming car
pace car (race car)
Packard
passenger car
pedal car
Peugeot
Pierce-Arrow
Plymouth
police car

save/keep/preserve
search/reveal/find
seasons/springtime/summer/autumn/
    winter
seeing/eyes/vision aids
self-concept/self-esteem
sequence/before/after/first/next/last
sets/pairs/groups/paired associations
sew/knit/weave/needlework
shake/vibrate/wiggle/fidget
shame/embarrassment/modesty
shape/form
sharp/pointed/tapered
shoes/boots/hosiery
signs/signals/warnings/alarms
simplify/reduce complexity
sit/recline/kneel
size/large/small
skin/complexion
sleep/dream/rest/tiredness
smell/nose/odors
smoking/cigarettes/tobacco use
soft/pliant/flexible
soil/sand/dust/powder/mud/erosion
Southeastern U.S./the South/Florida
Southwestern U.S./Southwest/Texas to
    Arizona
speaking/speeches/spoken
    communication
speed/fast/slow
spirals/twists/coils
sport fishing/commercial fishing
sports/athletics/coaching/sports teams
start/begin/establish
stop/end/cease
stores/shopping/buying
storms/hurricanes/tornadoes
streets/roads/trails/paths
stress/anxiety/frustration
strong/tough/durable/sturdy
structures/arenas/bridges/towers/tunnels
substance abuse/illicit drugs/alcohol
    abuse
substitute/replace
sun/sunshine/sunrise/sunset
surprise/amazement/the unexpected
swim/dive/swimming pools
systems/processes/methods

taste/flavor/seasonings
taxes/taxation
tech./engineering/inventions/prototypes
telecommunications/telephone/telegraph
temperature/hot/cold/heat/cool
tennis/racket sports
texture/smooth/rough/wrinkled
the theater/performing arts
thinking/intelligence/ignorance
throw/catch
time/timepieces/duration/brief/lengthy
tools/machinery
top/above/up
touch/feel/itch/rub/scrape
toys/dolls/puppets
training/practice/lessons
travel/vacations/tourism/resorts/hotels
trends/fads/popular taste
turn/roll/rotate/circle/twist/flip
TV/TV personalities
unfriendly/unkind/mean/antagonistic
United Kingdom/Ireland
unusual/rare/strange/odd/unique
U.S. government/presidency/legislation
vanity/pride/egotism/conceit
walk/run/step/crawl/march
walls/ceilings/roofs
warfare/military conquest
water/ice
water sports/surfing/water-skiing
weak/fragile/delicate/mild
wealth/luxury/opulence
weapons/ammunition
weather/climate/clouds/atmosphere
weight/heavy/light/fat/skinny
Western Europe/Scandinavia
Western U.S./the Rocky Mt. states
wet/dry
wheels/tires/gears
white/pale
width/thick/thin/broad/narrow
windows/window treatments
winter sports/skiing/ice-skating
wires/chains/cables/cords
wood/lumbering industry/forestry
yellow/orange
young adults/middle age

FIFTEEN

Word Bait Lures

Throughout *The IdeaFisher*, you have encountered a variety of questions—lures—that are closely associated with solving a specific problem. They have been consolidated and expanded here to include others in the same categories, as a quick reference guide when you're fishing for bigger Word Bait. The following questions have been selected from the IdeaFisher software and its modules. Therefore, they may be worded differently than in previous chapters.

Chapter Three
Word Bait Questions

1. What does this word make me think of?

2. How could I use this word—alone, some part of it, or combined with something else—to solve my problem?

Chapter Four
Defining the Problem Questions

1. What are you trying to accomplish? Consider:

   What is the problem? What is the challenge?
   What must be decided?

2. What if you were simply to ignore the situation? Might time alone solve the problem?

3. If it won't go away by itself: is the problem really worth solving?

   Who agrees that this is an important challenge, and why?

   Which relevant persons regard it as unimportant, and why?

   By solving the problem, what do you stand to gain?

What do others stand to lose?

What is the worst that can happen if the problem is not resolved?

4. What resources can you dedicate to reaching a solution?

5. How should decisions along the way to a solution be reached?

Who should be involved in arriving at decisions?

Who should make the final decision?

In what manner should decisions be made (such as unilaterally; by majority vote; by consensus)?

6. How will you know when you have achieved your purpose? What are your criteria of success? For example:

What will people be doing well? How will they feel about their work?

How will they be getting along with each other?

How will your own work be easier or more enjoyable?

What will you no longer have to attend to: What will you no longer be concerned about?

7. Regarding your own interest in the matter: what are your personal and professional reasons for working on this project?

What risks or threats must you face in solving this problem?

What is most fearsome or threatening about the problem itself?

What is it you fear losing the most if this problem is not resolved?

8. How strong is your personal commitment to the effort? Are you willing to invest the necessary time and energy?

Might you be overstimulated or too motivated to reach a conclusion?

How might this urgency affect the quality or ethics of your decision?

9. Whose problem is it?

Is it really your problem? What if you transfer responsibility?

10. When was the need or trouble first noticed? Did it occur suddenly, or had it been developing for some time before anyone noticed it?

How did it manifest itself? What were the symptoms or indicators that something needed attention?

11. How did you become aware of the situation?

When did you become aware of it? How do you feel about the timing or about the way you were informed?

What else do you know about the history of the problem?

12. What do you now understand about the cause or causes of the problem?

13. Why hasn't the problem already been solved?

14. What is the crux of the issue?

    To gain other perspectives so you don't solve the wrong problem:

    Who can give you a different perspective on the nature of the problem and the crux of the issue?

    Whose point of view should be considered because the person is affected by the problem?

    What if you also get the perspective of at least one person who appreciates the problem but who is not directly affected by it?

    What if you make believe that you are several different people, viewing the same set of facts from various perspectives (with different vested interests)?

15. What do you believe is the extent of the problem? (How pervasive or widespread is it?) What is its magnitude in numbers?:

    How quickly is the problem spreading or developing? What is the risk of time passing without resolution?

    What if you seek a temporary solution before a permanent one?

    Who can give you an unbiased perspective on the magnitude or seriousness of the problem (perhaps someone who has faced a similar challenge, or someone outside your domain)?

16. How complex is the problem?

    What other problems are linked with this one? How are they interrelated? For example:

    How does one problem lead to—or result from—another?
    What small problems add up to this big problem or make it worse?

17. If you're not fully aware of the assumptions guiding your work, why continue wearing blinders: Consider:

    Are you aiming at the right target? Are you working on the right problem?

    Have you oversimplified the problem?

    What are you taking for granted about the urgency of a solution?

    What if you just wait and see what happens?

    What do you assume are the givens that can't be changed? What if you change them anyway?

    What are you assuming to be impossible? What if you try it nevertheless?

    What procedures do you assume are necessary? What if you skip them?

    What "facts" have you assumed to be correct: How might their information fool you?

    What trouble can you redefine as an opportunity?

18. Have any of your answers to these questions changed your thinking about the subject?

    How has the challenge grown or expanded: What does it now encompass:

    Do you now see it as one problem or as several interrelated problems or sub-problems?

    What do you now think is the root cause of the problem, or what causes appear to be intermeshed?

    What do you now believe is the crux of the issue?

    Whose problem is it now? If it's not yours now, why stay involved?

    Considering the big picture, what about this problem is most important?

    What is the most difficult barrier to a satisfying solution?

    What is now your primary aim/goal/objective?

    What about the problem is most urgent or most in need of immediate attention?

19. How do these changes in your thinking affect the decisions that must be made?

    How do the changes in your thinking affect the manner in which decisions should be reached?

20. How confident are you that you have framed the central problem rather than a side issue or a false problem? (What is your level of confidence, such as "95 percent sure"?)

    How likely is it that the real problem will not be known until you have reached at least a partial solution?

21. What are your thoughts about a final deadline for reaching a satisfying conclusion?

22. Did your definition of the problem drastically change? If so return to the beginning of these questions and answer them again with your new perspective in mind.

23. Who else is engaged in trying to solve this problem?

    Who else should be involved? (What other groups, agencies, and individuals share your interest? Why should they participate?)

    How can you enlist their participation?

    Who is involved but should not be? Why is their participation not relevant or not helpful?

    Are any who are trying to solve this problem actually making it worse? (In what way? What happens?)

How can you change the efforts that are not appropriate or not helpful (as by remedial instruction, reassignment, removal from the project, or asking the people what they think)?

24. Whose attitude or behavior is the problem or part of the problem?

    What have other people done to perpetuate the situation? (Who has done what, or failed to do what: For what reason?)

    What have you done to perpetuate the situation?

25. Who has a vested interest in the status quo? How do they benefit from things as they are—and what do they think they'll lose if the problem is solved?

    Are those with a vested interest actually part of the problem?

    How likely is it that those with a vested interest will resist your efforts? What form might their resistance take?

    What thought have you given to mutual problem solving?

26. If the issue involves conflict between personal value systems: how are emotions interfering with efforts to find a solution?

27. What other emotions are interfering: For example:

    What negative emotions—such as anger, envy, resentment, mistrust, wounded pride, or protection of territory/turf—are affecting the attitudes of those whose help you need?

    How are the feelings expressed in people's behavior?

    What positive attitudes might also be interfering (such as conscientiousness, or extreme loyalty to company/colleagues)?

    How are the attitudes expressed in people's behavior?

    How important is it to deal with the positive and negative feelings before you forge ahead? What though have you given to the way this might be done?

28. If this is primarily a "people problem" or if someone's "misconduct" is of central concern: what is the nature of the behavior, and who is engaged in it?

    To whom is the behavior objectionable, and for what reason?

    What appears to be the purpose of the "misconduct"? (To gain attention? To win a power struggle? To seek revenge?)

    To check your analysis: how does the recipient of this behavior feel when the person behaves this way? (Irritated? Challenged? Defeated? Hurt?)

    What other payoffs does the "perpetrator" gain from this behavior?

    What do you think the person is trying to say about himself or herself by engaging in this conduct (such as I'm powerful . . . I'm brave . . . I'm smarter than you . . . I'm important . . . I need help)?

29. Who else do you think may be contributing to the behavior by egging it on or approving of it?

    What satisfaction or reward do those in the background gain by tolerating or contributing to the "misconduct"?

30. What efforts have been made to stop or modify the behavior? (Who has done what with whom?)

    How does the person respond to your efforts to stop the behavior?

    What happens when you steadfastly ignore it?

    What happens when you allow logical consequences to take their course (such as allowing the person to experience failure, rather than rescuing or covering for the person)?

    Could this be an opportunity to address this person?

Chapter Five
Six Universal Questions

1. Who?	4. When?
2. What?	5. Why?
3. Where?	6. How?

Chapter Seven
Strategic Planning Questions

1. What qualifies a person as a prospective customer for this product/service?

   What purchasing power?

   What decision-making power?

   What degree of interest?

   How quickly should the person be able to reach a decision?

2. Who most often makes the decision to buy this type of product/service? Is it the person who will be using it?

   Who else influences the purchasing process (such as a gatekeeper)?

   Who is the end user?

3. What problem is the customer trying to solve, for which the product/service is a solution?

   As you analyze the customer's problem what clues do you gather about the product benefits you should stress? What clues about product/service features to point out?

4. Over the past couple of years, what changes have you noticed in your customers? For example:

What changes in discretionary income?

What changes in knowledge, education, sophistication, awareness?

What new interests?

What new worries?

What new expectations about products/services? For instance:

How has their definition of "quality" changed?

What former luxury is now considered a necessity? Or what former "extra" do customers now expect as a matter of course? Does this give you a clue to their future expectations?

5. How might your customers continue to change, and why?

How do you expect them to change, and why?

What provisions should you make in preparation for the changes?

6. Which type of customer should be your first priority in planning, and why?

Should your emphasis be on attracting the customer, keeping the customer, or both?

7. Which type of customer should be your second priority in planning, and why?

Where should you place your emphasis?

8. Which type of customer should be your third priority in planning, and why?

Where should you place your emphasis?

9. Whom do you expect your choicest customer to be five years from now? Ten years from now, and beyond?

10. What is the "lifetime value" of a customer?

11. How would you describe the relationship you've developed with your customers?

What can you do to strengthen this relationship?

12. How loyal are your customers? How many think of you as their supplier and would rather do business with you than with anyone else?

How many repeat customers do you have, and why do they return?

What purchase pattern or behavior pattern have you noticed among your repeat customers?

13. What can you do to encourage greater loyalty? Such as:

differentiate your product/service or company more clearly from the competition

do a better job of targeting a niche market

make customer satisfaction a priority; follow through with better service

listen to your customers more carefully; show them greater interest and appreciation

14. How many new customers have you gained during the past year?

    Why have they decided to do business with you?

15. How many customers have you lost, and what have been their real reasons for dropping you? How do you know?

    How can the loss of customers be prevented?

16. What general dissatisfaction have customers expressed, and what is your source of information?

17. Do you have a recent study of customer satisfaction? Why or why not?

    If you've not formally inquired about customer satisfaction: what would you want to find out?

    Would the information be worth the expense?

18. What have your customers been asking for recently?

    Which customer requests seem to hold the greatest potential?

19. Do prospective customers already understand this product, or do you also have to sell them on the idea behind it?

    If marketing is an educational process: how do you know that your prospects are ready and willing to be educated?

20. Integrating what you know of the customer's needs and traits, what product/service benefits and features would you say are most meaningful to your customer? Such as:

    comfort, convenience, safety, design, efficiency, newness, power, speed, quality, size, status, service after purchase

21. What does the customer's philosophy of life or value system suggest about things to avoid mentioning?

    What images or features might turn the customer off?

22. Considering all you know about the customer's psychology, how appropriate is the tone of your message?

23. From the customer's standpoint, what are the best improvements you could make in customer service and satisfaction?

24. How could you get customers involved in using a service regularly?

25. How well does your current customer service live up to its name?

26. Do you have a "secret shopper" program to check on customer satisfaction?

27. In what different ways do various customers use your product/service?

28. For this kind of product/service what is the competitive environment?

29. What are their competitive strengths and weaknesses?

30. What peripheral companies might you have overlooked as competitors?

31. How are your most successful competitors alike?

32. What is the worst that your competition might do to you?

33. Could you form a strategic alliance with other companies to help lower the impact of this?

34. Which of your competitor's services could you copy or adapt to your own situation?

35. What other forms of your product/service exist?

Chapter Nine
Speech Questions

1. Why will the audience be there?

   mainly to learn something they can use

   mainly to socialize, or to see and be seen

   mainly to be entertained

   mainly to be inspired or persuaded

   mainly to fulfill a duty

   it's a captive audience; they have no choice

2. If you'll be sharing the stage with other speakers, what do you expect their presentations to be?

   What topics will other speakers give?

   Any views that oppose or contradict your own?

   What presentation styles will other speakers give—serious, humorous, dragging, fast-paced, superdynamic, direct, story-telling?

3. What do you expect their attitude will be toward the material you present?

   curious, eager to learn

   skeptical, critical

   open-minded, receptive to different opinions

   threatened, defensive if challenged

   not interested

noncommittal, difficult to read

4. What forms of evidence will be most convincing to this audience? What kinds of specifics do they respond to?

examples; statistics; definitions; hard facts; details

direct comparisons and contrasts

indirect comparisons (analogies, metaphors)

testimonials and quotations

human-interest stories

results of experiments; case studies

models, prototypes; simulations; role play

actual hands-on experience

5. What, if any, topic have you been assigned?

What, if any, goal have you been assigned?

6. Exactly what is the concern, or the issue of common interest, around which you will build this speech?

Is it the heart of the matter (what you might call a burning issue or a root cause of concern), or is it not so fundamental?

If you're not addressing a fundamental interest: what is the burning issue, and why not build your case around it?

7. What different angle or slant on the subject (what premise; what point of view) will you use to get and keep the attention of the audience?

8. Exactly what do you want your speech to accomplish?

As a result of your speech, what do you want the audience to understand?

What new point of view, or what different perspective, do you want the audience to gain?

What attitude toward a subject do you want them to hold?

What skill do you want them to acquire?

What conclusion do you want them to reach?

What do you want them to do as a result of your presentation?

What could move this group to take such action?

9. What few (not more than five) main points should you use to build your case?

Main Point #1:

Main Point #2:

Main Point #3:

Main Point #4:

Main Point #5:

10. If you're presenting more than one main point: what type of sequence would be the clearest, the most persuasive, and the best for leading up to a climax?

    sequence in chronological order

      according to the passage of time

      step by step

    sequence in topical order

      from least to most important

      from easiest to most difficult

      from least to most surprising/dramatic

    sequence in spatial order

      according to places/location

      according to parts of a whole

    sequence according to your preferred mode of problem solving

11. Beginning your chosen sequence: which main point will be the first one presented?

    What evidence/benefits/other specifics can support or clarify it?

    What transitional comment can connect this point to the next one?

12. Which will be the second main point?

    What evidence/benefits/other specifics can support or clarify it?

    What transitional comment can connect this point to the next one?

13. Which will be the third main point?

    What evidence/benefits/other specifics can support or clarify it?

    What transitional comment can connect this point to the next one?

14. Which will be the fourth main point?

    What evidence/benefits/other specifics can support or clarify it?

    What transitional comment can connect this point to the next one?

15. Which will be the fifth main point?

    What evidence/benefits/other specifics can support or clarify it?

    What do your points all lead up to?

16. In light of your different slant on the subject and the points you've made to support it, what will you present as your conclusion (your proposal/package/product/plan)?

If you've not already identified the benefits, what does the audience stand to gain by adopting this conclusion?

17. To begin tying your presentation together, create a quick preview introducing the core of your message:

    What is an interesting way to let the audience know what your presentation is about (your central idea; what you're going to tell them)?

    Optional: Briefly include the main points you're going to make.

18. To continue tying your presentation together, create a quick review summarizing your central idea. (Tell them what you've told them).

    What phrase or sentence would be an effective transition from the body of the message to the quick review (between the conclusion and the summary statement)?

19. To open your speech, what should be the very first words out of your mouth? (What would be the most fitting and effective attention-getter pertaining to the heart of your message?)

    a call for audience participation or response

    a gimmick for shock value

    a reference to a historic event

    a relevant joke; a pun

    a relevant quotation

    a specific compliment for the audience

    a startling fact or statistic

    a stimulating question

    an amusing true story; a touching true story

    an example or an illustration

20. Should your attention-getter be serious, amusing, or tragicomic?

    If you're the first speaker and there is no emcee: what sort of attention-getter can also warm up the audience?

    How much time should you spend on the attention-getter, as compared with the rest of the speech?

21. What phrase or sentence would be an effective transition connecting the attention-getter to the brief preview of your message?

22. To close your speech after the quick review, what should be the very last words out of your mouth?

    What similar wording could tie the close to the attention-grabber opener?

    If you opened with a joke, how about repeating it with a different punch line?

If you opened with a quotation, how about ending with the line that follows it?

If you opened with a remarkable fact, what if you project that into the future?

What is the most memorable statement you could make in reference to the heart of your message?

What if you close with a reference to the theme of the program or to the subject of the speaker?

What if you end with a call to action?

What specific next step should the audience take and by what date should they get it done?

23. What phrase or sentence would be an effective transition connecting the quick review to the close you have just created?

24. What tangible material can you leave behind for the audience to remember you by?

an outline on which they can make notes as you speak

a handout such as a summary or a checklist

a copy of an article you have published

promotional material

a copy of a proposal

Chapter Eleven
Modify Questions

1. What are the components of your idea?

2. What if you make the appearance more important than the quality?

3. What if you make appearance less important than it is?

4. What if you were to change the character of a physical sensation?

5. What if the appearance were changed superficially?

6. What if you were to change a different visual quality, such as a partial view?

7. What if you linked different sensations such as color-shape or color-sound?

8. What if its appearance were to symbolize something?

9. What if its appearance mimicked something else?

10. What if it appealed to a different social group such as conservative or avante-garde?

11. What if you make it more expensive or extravagant?

12. What if its features were surprising?

13. What if its appearances were deceiving, like an optical illusion or a mirage?

14. What if its appearance were variable as in a change of costumes or wigs?

15. What if its appearance were to alter with the passage of time such as in the changing of the seasons?

16. What if it were quickly to change form?

17. What if it were to switch identities back and forth?

18. What if its appearance were distorted?

19. How would it appear through a colored filter?

20. What if you change the size?

21. What if you change the shape?

22. What if you change the texture?

23. What if you use the analogy of a fashion collection?

24. What if a temperature change were to affect the appearance?

25. What if it looked more high tech?

26. What if it looked simpler or less intimidating?

27. What if you express an idea more graphically?

28. What if you caricaturize a person?

29. What is the most surprising or outrageous way in which you could modify the physical appearance?

30. What if you simply combine one or more current purposes?

31. What if you combine different functions as in a body part with more than one function?

32. What if you borrow features of two or more categories of products and services, like combining tools in a Swiss army knife?

33. What if some parts were interchangeable?

34. What if you were to design a single piece to take the place of several?

35. What if you borrow principles or processes from another discipline such as archaeology or detective work?

36. What if you bring out visual harmony?

37. What if all or part of it were a rendition of a basic shape such as a diamond?

38. If it's two-dimensional, could you make it three-dimensional or make it appear three-dimensional?

39. What if you could provide it in assorted shapes?

40. What if it were twisted, braided, or intertwined?

41. What if it were angled or sharply bent?

42. What shape would it be if you flipped it over?

43. What if it could change identity by assuming different shapes such as a Transformer toy?

44. What if it were to lose its shape?

45. What if the texture were changed?

46. What if it were distorted?

47. What if a component that is normally on the top were on the bottom?

    What if a component that is normally on the bottom were on the top?

48. What if any of these components could function alone or in some combination with another?

49. What if certain materials maintained their own identities?

50. What if you softened something about it?

51. What if you joined forces with another group?

52. What is the most irrational arrangement you can think of?

53. What if you placed something back-to-back?

54. What could you learn by creating a model of your idea?

Chapter Eleven
Evaluate Questions

1. What difficulties do you foresee in putting your idea into practice?

2. Who else could give valid advice about feasibility and implementation?

3. If you think your goal is not attainable as stated, what would be a satisfactory alternative?

4. What spin-offs does your idea already suggest?

5. How does it lend itself to adaptation for other audiences, such as older people, younger people, or people of the opposite sex?

6. What parts of your idea can be used to solve other problems?

7. What are the major strengths of your idea?

8. What are the major weaknesses of your idea?

9. On a scale of one to ten, how original, how novel, how fresh is your idea?

10. Has something like this existed before?

11. How is this version more suitable for the times?

12. Which of the following groups of positive descriptors could a critic apply to your idea, and why?

intriguing, absorbing, engrossing, gripping, fascinating

stimulating, stirring, awakening, piquing, provocative

thrilling, electrifying

spirited, animated, sparkly, spunky, zestful, lively, bright

palatable, appetizing

tangy, spicy, fiery, peppery, savory, gingerly

amusing, diverting, entertaining

learned, erudite, informative, well-informed

inspiring, enlightening; visionary

significant, important; monumental

relevant, helpful

13. Which of the following groups of negative descriptors could a critic apply to your idea, and why?

insipid, bland, mild, blank; no personality

vapid, stale, flat, lifeless; no spirit, sparkle, or tang

barren, arid, meager, unable to satisfy the hunger of the mind

banal, tasteless, trivial, platitudinous, truistic

ordinary, obvious, pedestrian, uninspired

wishy-washy, limp-wristed, weak, diluted

inane, purposeless, pointless, devoid of significance

stupid, asinine, unintelligent

irksome, tiresome, wearisome

dull, humdrum, dreary, monotonous, repetitive

pedantic, heavy, stodgy, bookish, overly exacting

slow, plodding

irrelevant; unhelpful

14. Is your idea similar to something else?

15. How closely have you met the criteria of an "elegant" idea?

Is it precise?

Is it neat?

Is it simple?

Does the idea "feel right"?

16. How easy is your idea to understand? Could you explain it in 25 words or less?

17. Does your idea improve ease of maintenance?

18. How does your idea affect someone's quality of life?

    How does it affect safety?
    How does it affect physical comfort?

19. What overt or subtle stereotypes are embodied in your idea, such as that of highly educated people?

20. How easy is your idea to use?

21. How sure are you that you are fully aware of what appeals to this marketplace?

22. Realistically, what evidence do you have that this concept will succeed?

23. Is the customer willing to pay the asking price?

24. What subgoals does it already suggest?

25. Imagine yourself in the future looking back on your current decisions. What would you think you did right?

Bibliography

Adams, James L. *The Care and Feeding of Ideas*. Reading, Mass.: Addison-Wesley Publishing Co., 1986.

Albrecht, Karl. *Brain Power*. Englewood Cliffs, N.J.: Prentice Hall, Inc., 1980

Albrecht, Karl. *The Creative Corporation*. Homewood, Ill.: Dow Jones–Irwin, 1987.

Allen, Myron S. *Morphological Creativity*. Englewood Cliffs, N.J.: Prentice Hall, Inc., 1962.

Brondi, Angelo M. *Have an Affair with Your Mind*. Great Neck, N.Y.: Creative Synergetic Association, Ltd., 1973.

Buzan, Tony. *The Brain User's Guide*. New York, N.Y.: E. P. Dutton, Inc., 1983.

Buzan, Tony. *Make the Most of Your Mind*. New York, N.Y.: Simon & Schuster, 1994.

Bandrowski, James F. *Corporate Imagination Plus*. New York, N.Y.: The Free Press, 1990.

Cell, Edward. *Learning to Learn from Experience*. Albany, N.Y.: State University of New York Press, 1984.

Costa, Arthur L. *Developing Minds*. Roseville, Calif.: Arthur L. Costa, 1985.

Crawford, Robert P. *The Techniques of Creative Thinking*. Burlington, Vt.: Fraser Publishing Co., 1954.

Crawford, Robert P. *Direct Creativity*. Burlington, Vt.: Fraser Publishing Co., 1964.

Davis, Gary A. *Creativity Is Forever*. Dubuque, Iowa: Kendall/Hunt Publishing Co., 1983.

de Bono, Edward. *Lateral Thinking*. New York, N.Y.: Harper & Row, 1970.

Denette, Daniel C. *Brainstorms*. Cambridge, Mass.: The MIT Press, 1985.

Denning, Melita, and Osborne Phillips. *Creative Visualization*. St. Paul, Minn.: Llewellyn Publications, 1980.

Eden, Colin. *Messing About in Problems*. New York, N.Y.: Pergamon Press, 1983.

Edwards, Morris O. *Idea Power*. Buffalo, N.Y.: Bearly Limited, 1986.

Estes, W. K. *Handbook of Learning and Cognitive Processes*. New York, N.Y.: John Wiley & Sons, 1978.

Faburn, Don. *You and Creativity*. Beverly Hills, Calif.: Glencoe Press, 1968.

Flesch, Rudolf. *The Art of Readable Writing*. New York, N.Y.: Harper, 1949.

Gardner, Howard. *Frames of the Mind*. New York, N.Y.: Basic Books, Inc., 1985.

Gates, Elmer. *Art of Mind-Using*. New York, N.Y.: Exposition Press, 1971.

Gates, Elmer. *Originality & Invention Applied to Livelihood & Business*. Star Route, Due West, S.C.: Elmer Gates Institute of Psychurgy, 1981.

Glass, Arnold Lewis. *Cognition*. Reading, Mass.: Addison-Wesley Publishing Co., 1979.

Guilford, J. P. *Way Beyond the I.Q*. Buffalo, N.Y.: The Creative Education Foundation, 1977.

Hampden-Turner, Charles. *Maps of the Mind*. New York, N.Y.: Collier Books, 1981.

Harman, Willis, and Howard Rheingold. *Higher Creativity*. Boston, Mass.: Houghton Mifflin Co., 1984.

Haugeland, John. *Artificial Intelligence*. Cambridge, Mass.: The MIT Press, 1985.

Hayes, John R. *Cognitive Psychology*. Homewood, Ill.: The Dorsey Press, 1978.

Hayes, John R. *The Complete Problem Solver*. Philadelphia, Pa.: The Franklin Institute, 1981.

Heimbold, Noreen, and Jim Betts. *New Products*. Point Pleasant, N.J.: Point Publishing Co., 1984.

Hintzman, Douglas L. *The Psychology of Learning & Memory*. San Francisco, Calif.: W. H. Freeman & Co., 1978.

Holland, John. *Induction*. Cambridge, Mass.: The MIT Press, 1986.

Isaksen, Scott G. *Frontiers of Creativity Research*. Buffalo, N.Y.: Bearly Limited, 1987.

James, William. *Talks to Teachers*. New York, N.Y.: W. W. Norton & Company, Inc., 1900.

John-Steiner, Vera. *Notebooks of the Mind*. New York, N.Y.: Harper & Row, 1985.

Kaufman, Roger. *Identifying and Solving Problems; A Systems Approach*. San Diego, Calif.: University Associates, 1986.

Khatena, Joe. *Imagery & Creative Imagination*. Buffalo, N.Y.: Bearly Limited, 1934.

Killeffer, David H. *How Did You Think of That?* Washington, D.C.: American Chemical Society, 1973.

Kim, Steven H. *Essence of Creativity*. New York, N.Y.: Oxford University Press, 1990.

Kubie, Lawrence S. *Neurotic Distortion of the Creative Process*. New York, N.Y.: Farrar, Straus and Giroux, 1958.

Kuhn, Robert Lawrence. *Handbook for Creative and Innovative Managers*. New York, N.Y.: McGraw-Hill Book Company, 1988.

LaBeouf, Michael. *Imagineering*. New York, N.Y.: McGraw-Hill Book Co., 1982.

Litvak, Stuart B. *Use Your Head*. Englewood Cliffs, N.J.: Prentice Hall, Inc., 1982.

McCormac, Earl R. *A Cognitive Theory of Metaphor*. London, England: The MIT Press, 1985.

MacKinnon, Donald W. *In Search of Human Effectiveness*. Buffalo, N.Y.: Creative Education Foundation, Inc., 1978.

McCorduck, Pamela. *Machines Who Think*. New York, N.Y.: W. H. Freeman & Co., 1956.

Mattimore, Bryan W. *99% Inspiration*. New York, N.Y.: American Management Association, 1994.

May, Rollow. *The Courage to Create*. Toronto, Canada: Bantam Books, 1975.

Mayer, Richard E. *Thinking, Problem Solving, Cognition*. New York, N.Y.: W. H. Freeman & Co., 1947.

Mayer, Richard E. *Thinking and Problem Solving*. Glenview, Ill.: Scott, Foresman & Co., 1977.

Michalko, Michael. *Thinkertoys*. Berkeley, Calif.: Ten Speed Press, 1991.

Miller, William C. *The Creative Edge*. Reading, Mass.: Addison-Wesley Publishing Co., Inc., 1986.

Minsky, Marvin. *The Society of Mind*. New York, N.Y.: Simon & Schuster, 1986.

Nadler, Gerald, and Shozo Hibino. *Breakthrough Thinking*. Rocklin, Calif.: Prima Publishing, 1994.

Nayak, P. Ranganath, and Ketteringham. *Breakthroughs!* New York, N.Y.: Rawson Associates, 1986.

Norman, Donald A. *Things That Make Us Smart*. Reading, Mass.: Addison-Wesley Publishing Co., 1993.

Olson, Robert W. *The Art of Creative Thinking*. New York, N.Y.: Harper & Row, 1978.

Osborne, Alex F. *Applied Imagination*. New York, N.Y.: Charles Scribner's Sons, 1979.

Parnes, Sidney. *The Magic of Your Mind*. Buffalo, N.Y.: Bearly Limited, 1981.

Perkins, D. N. *The Mind's Best Work*. Cambridge, Mass.: Harvard University Press, 1981.

Raudsepp, Eugene. *Creative Growth Games*. New York, N.Y.: Perigee Books, 1977.

Raudsepp, Eugene. *How Creative Are You?* New York, N.Y.: G. A. Putnam's Sons, 1981.

Raudsepp, Eugene. *How to Create New Ideas*. Englewood Cliffs, N.J.: Prentice Hall, Inc., 1982.

Rawlinson, J. Geoffrey. *Creative Thinking and Brainstorming*. Guldford and King's Lynn, England: Biddles Ltd., 1983.

Ray, Michael, and Rochelle Myers. *Creativity in Business*. New York, N.Y.: Doubleday, 1986.

Rosenau, Milton D., Jr. *Innovation*. Belmont, Calif.: Lifetime Learning Publications, 1982.

Russell, Peter. *The Brain Book*. New York, N.Y.: E. P. Dutton, Inc., 1979.

Sanders, Donald A. and Judith A. *Teaching Creativity Through Metaphor*. New York, N.Y.: Longman, 1984.

Samples, Bob. *The Metaphoric Mind*. Reading, Mass.: Addison-Wesley Publishing Co., 1976.

Sharkey, N. E. *Advances in Cognitive Science*. New York, N.Y.: John Wiley & Sons, 1986.

Thornburg, David D. *Unlocking Personal Creativity*. Los Altos, Calif.: Innovision, 1986.

Titchener, E. B. *Lectures on the Experimental Psychology of the Thought-Processes*. New York, N.Y.: Macmillan, 1909.

Torrance, E. Paul. *The Search for Satori & Creativity*. Buffalo, N.Y.: Creative Education Foundation, Inc., 1979.

Upton, Albert. *Design for Thinking*. Palo Alto, Calif.: Pacific Books, 1941.

Upton, Albert. *Creative Analysis*. New York, N.Y.: E. P. Dutton, 1961.

Vaughan, Francis E. *Awakening Intuition*. Garden City, N.Y.: Anchor Books, 1979.

Van Gundy, Arthur B. *Training Your Creative Mind*. Englewood Cliffs, N.J.: Prentice Hall, Inc., 1982.

Van Gundy, Arthur B. *108 Ways to Get a Bright Idea*. Englewood Cliffs, N.J.: Prentice Hall, Inc., 1983.

Weber, Robert J. *Forks, Phonographs & Hot Air Balloons*. New York, N.Y.: Oxford University Press, 1992.

Wonder, Jacquelyn, and Priscilla Donovan. *Whole Brain Thinking*. New York, N.Y.: William Morrow & Co., 1984.

Young, James Webb. *A Technique for Producing Ideas*. Chicago: Crain Communications, Inc., 1975.

Young, John G. *S-E-L-E-C-T: Creative/Innovative Approaches*. Buffalo, N.Y.: Bearly Limited, 1986.

Zdenek, Marilee. *The Right-Brain Experience*. New York, N.Y.: McGraw-Hill Book Company, 1983.

About the Author and Inventor

The son of sharecroppers, Marsh Fisher was born and raised in Pleasant Valley, Iowa. Along with his parents and two younger brothers, he worked on the farm and helped run a country store that occupied the front room of their two-room house.

Marsh left the farm via the Air Force, becoming a B-25 pilot during World War II while still a teenager. After the war, he received a bachelor's degree from the University of Colorado and moved to Hong Kong, where he worked for the travel division of American Express. Returning to the states, Marsh was appointed the sales manager for Fisher Pen Company and formed his own vocal trio, The Boys Next Door. The group recorded for the RCA label and became regulars on the Arthur Godfrey Show.

Next, Marsh moved to California and took up real estate sales. In 1970, he developed the idea for what would become the world's largest real estate sales organization. One year later he and his partner, Art Bartlett, started Century 21 Real Estate Corporation with $6000 in capital.

Since retiring in 1977, Marsh has dedicated himself and his resources to the development of the IdeaFisher software program which annually automates a part of the thinking process. The program's more than 700,000 linked entries allows users instant access to information directly related to any problem they're trying to solve. As of this writing, the program's add-on modules of task-specific questions include the Strategic Planning Module, Public Relations Module, Creative Writing Module, Business & Grant Proposal Module, Consultant's Module, Speech & Presentation Module, and Conflict Resolution Module.

Marsh and his wife, Marlee, reside in Newport Beach, California.

For further information regarding the IdeaFisher software program, contact IdeaFisher Systems, Inc., at 2222 Martin Street, Suite 110, Irvine, CA 92715, (800) 289-4332, (714) 474-8111, or Fax (714) 474-1778.